FORMING
STORMING NORMING
PERFORMING

FORMING
STORMING NORMING
PERFORMING

Successful Communication in Groups And Teams

Donald B. Egolf, Ph.D.

Writers Club Press
San Jose New York Lincoln Shanghai

FORMING STORMING NORMING PERFORMING
Successful Communication in Groups And Teams

Writers Club Press
an imprint of iUniverse, Inc.

For information address:
iUniverse, Inc.
5220 S. 16th St., Suite 200
Lincoln, NE 68512
www.iuniverse.com

ISBN: 0-595-20444-9

Printed in the United States of America

Preface

In 1965 Bruce Tuckman published an article on the developmental sequences in small groups. In the article Tuckman reviewed the works of a number of researchers who studied the developmental stages or phases of small group development. In synthesizing the reviewed researchers' works, Tuckman proposed that groups proceed through four general stages of development. Tuckman named those stages: *forming, storming, norming,* and *performing.*

I have found the content in Tuckman's article to be very useful in teaching undergraduates over the years. His synthesis was well reasoned and comprehensive. In addition, the use of the mnemonic of rhyme in naming the stages was extremely clever. In talking with undergraduates that I had in my classes years ago the number who remember and recite the mantra of *forming, storming, norming,* and *performing* is amazing. I often thought that if I should ever write a book on small group and team communication I would use Tuckman's rhyme as the lead title for the book. So now that time has come.

I dedicate this book to all the undergraduates that I have taught, am currently teaching, and will teach. May you always be out there *forming, storming, norming,* and *performing.*

CHAPTER 1

THE BASICS

Few of us are truly independent. We rely upon the cooperation of others for the completion of tasks and for making decisions. In addition, interaction with others is crucial in the acquisition and maintenance of a self-concept. Through interacting with others, we satisfy our social needs and create a social reality. The completion of tasks, the making of decisions, the acquisition and maintenance of self-concept, and the creation of a social reality often occur in a group setting. It is the communication within this setting that is the focus of this book.

The study of small group and team communication is important because it is experienced by virtually everyone. In fact, every reader of this book has had at least some experience in the area and, therefore, has some degree of expertise. And, if the currently popular human relations expert,

1

Tom Peters, is correct, all of us will have much more such experiences in the future:

> Now, all the value-added in the economy is based on knowledge, and you do not do brain work in groups of thousands; you do it in duos and trios, quartets and quintets, maybe 25s and 50s. In 1900, 50% of Americans were self-employed; by 1970, only 7% of us were. That's going to turn out to have been the anomalous period. The only security in a world where job security is gone is that your skills are better and your network richer at the end of this year than they were at the beginning. Your ability to improve your skill base and make yourself more marketable, whether you are a teamster or a neurosurgeon, is the only thing you've got. What skills will be required for tomorrow? Nobody knows. The important thing is to keep acquiring new ones (Peters, 1993, p. 44).

As Peters also reminds us, we will, in the future, continually need to sharpen our skills. One area of skill sharpening is communication and, specifically, small group and team communication. Therefore, it is hoped that reading this book will vastly increase your understanding of small group and team communication phenomena; will improve your small group communication skills; will help you to serve better as both leaders and followers in future small group and team situations; and will enable you to better understand the reasons for group successes and failures.

[handwritten margin note: purpose of the book]

Definitions

To get involved in issues of definition Durant has said,

> *"...lets loose the dogs of philosophic war. For nothing is so difficult as definition, nor any thing so severe a test and exercise of mental clarity and skill" (Will Durant, 1974, p. 16).*

Durant, in discussing the debate between Cephalus and Socrates about the meaning of "justice," reminds us that defining a concept or term, which is an attempt at clarity, can lead to controversy. Only in a comparatively few cases is there universal agreement on the meaning of a term, inches, pounds, meters, and liters, for example. In most cases definitions are arguable. People disagree on the meaning of art, communication, jazz, leadership, group, and team, for instance. The bases for their disagreements are not necessarily nefarious. People have different experiences, needs, and points of view that can motivate them to adopt different definitions.

This preamble is provided to pave the way for the definitions presented below. Although all scholars in the field may not agree upon the definitions, commonalities with other published definitions certainly exist.

Small Group

> A *small group* consists of three to nine individuals who have a common goal or purpose and who meet and communicate in a given medium for a period of time to achieve that goal or purpose.

This characterization of a small group reveals the definitional criteria of number, goal or purpose, meeting, communication, duration, and achievement. The rationale for the criteria follow.

The *number* range for a small group is three to nine. This range is somewhat at variance with some scholars, notably Goffman (1959), Fisher (1974), and Peters (1993). Goffman discusses a group of one, while Fisher and Peters put the upper limit at 20 and 25 respectively. The general reasoning for placing the number range from three to nine is that in this range the dynamics of small group communication are most manifest. More specific reasons for the three to nine number range will be presented below.

To be a group the members must share a *common goal* or *purpose.* The purpose may seem trivial or gravitas. For example, the purpose of the bowling group each Thursday night with your friends might simply be to have fun. Or, a medical review board might be meeting for the purpose of deciding which one of an array of critically-ill patients should be given the one available donor heart.

Meeting and *communicating* in a given *medium* are the next definitional requirements of a group. Meetings can be in the face-to-face medium or through electronic media. More and more small group meetings are being conducted via electronic media and even more will be so conducted in the future. Whatever the media, the *sine qua non* of small group communication is, of course, communication. Quite simply, no group purpose can be achieved without communication.

Duration is the final definitional criterion. A group needs a given period of time to achieve its purpose or goal. Indeed, the time period may be quite transient. A collection of strangers in an elevator may suddenly become a group when the elevator stalls and they are temporarily stranded. Broken from their frozen-forward and floor-number-directed gazes the elevator occupants begin to communicate. There may be the usual jokes, but talk eventually focuses on rescue. "Push the emergency call button," "Release the emergency phone," and so on. Most groups, of course, exist for much longer periods of time and some, like one's immediate family, for a lifetime.

Team

A *team* is a special type of small group and, therefore, must meet all the definitional criteria of a small group listed above. The special requirements that make a small group a team are that team members must have complementary skills, they must be accountable for their actions, and they will disband when they have achieved their purpose or goal.

That team members must have *complementary skills* means that each must have a skill the others do not, but the skill possessed must complement the skills of other members. For example, if you want to purchase a house you might assemble a team of an attorney, a financial agent (usually someone from a bank), and a house inspector. Here each proposed member would bring something to the table not possessed by the others. The goal, of course, is to acquire the house on your terms. The attorney is to make sure that the deed to the house is free and clear of liens, encumbrances, etc; the financial agent is to secure the funds for the purchase; and the inspector's role is to report on the structural integrity and safety of the house and whether it harbors any infestations or toxins.

Team members are *accountable*. In the home purchasing example above, the team is legally liable for its actions. The home purchaser has the legal recourse to sue the team or any of its members if the team performance is inadequate. If, after the purchase, the home purchaser discovers that there were liens against the property, that the interest compounding on the loan was misrepresented, and that the house was infested with termites, then legal action against the team would be justified. In short, a team is accountable for its actions.

Finally, a team *disbands* when it reaches its goal. When the team of the attorney, financial representative, and home inspector take their client, the purchaser, to a successful closing, they have reached their goal and they disband. The life span of a team, therefore, is much shorter than that of many other groups. The advantage to this shorter longevity is that the team does not suffer from the sclerotic processes that hamper other groups. One such process is *groupthink* wherein group cohesiveness becomes paramount and critical thinking suffers. Moreover, groups not refreshed with new members often suffer from a cognitive rigidity that prevents them from producing creative solutions even when the group has the best intentions. In longstanding groups, meetings often become predictable and boring. In contrast, in newly-constituted teams, meetings can be surprising and exciting. There, of course, can be a creative tension between teams and longstanding groups. The team can produce new, creative, and brash ideas that the longstanding group will see as unworkable. Contention between these two positions might lead to a third and perhaps superior position. Or it might lead to the weakening or demise of the parent organization.

"Team" as it is used here is a sports metaphor. It carries with it the notion that winning and losing are team concerns and the realization that every position or player and teamwork are important, for instance. And non-athletic teams often use locker room wall slogans to motivate and remind: "There is no 'I' in team. There is no 'U' in team. Winning isn't everything. It's the only thing."

The Context of Small Group Communication

One common way of categorizing human communication is on the dimension of number. This categorization scheme produces five types of communication: self- or intrapersonal communication, interpersonal communication, small group and team communication, public communication, and mass communication.

Self- or *intrapersonal communication* is communication with one's self. One is both the sender and the receiver. When we think, worry, remember, dream, daydream, and fantasize we are self-communicating. Self-communication is virtually unstoppable. Even when we sleep the dream videotape is running. Even when vigilance to external stimuli is required, there are still lapses into self-communication, sometimes related to external stimuli and at other times divorced from those stimuli. Self-communication is important in planning and ordering our lives, in thinking about ideals, in creating, and in escaping into fantasyland when the demands of the world become too burdensome.

Interpersonal communication is communication in the two-person, usually face-to-face setting. Common interpersonal pairings are parent-child, best friends, spouses, colleagues, superior-subordinate, and so on.

Interpersonal communication is very important in the establishment and maintenance of a positive self-concept. This has been referred to as the *Looking Glass Self.* Involved in the looking glass self is the fact that others in our environment are always giving us feedback in response to our appearance and actions. They are in a sense acting like a mirror reflecting their attitudes and feelings toward us. These reflections affect us. The reflections can make us feel worthy and valued, leading to a positive self-concept, or the reflections can be negative and make us feel unworthy and not valued, leading to a negative self-concept.

Small group communication is communication among three to nine individuals. Something very dramatic happens when the number of inter-actants increases from two to three. First, *coalitions* can form. Two individuals can form a coalition against the third. This is the *two-against-one* phenomenon. At least three people are needed for this phenomenon to occur. With just two individuals no coalitions can form. Coalitions even in the three-person group can and do change. At one point Persons A and B can form a coalition against C, but later, Persons B and C can form a coalition against Person A. This tendency to form coalitions is a key dynamic characteristic of small groups.

Second, when number changes from two to three, there is a basic change in communication behavior. When Person A is talking to Person B in the presence of Person C it is no longer interpersonal communication. Why? Because Person C is there to hear the exchange. Therefore, in a group, speakers continually edit their messages for the group even though those messages may ostensibly be addressed to a given member of the group. At times Person A may seem to be talking to Person B but in reality the message may be intended for Person C. Freud reported an example of this when he was counseling one of his patients and realized that he was actually addressing the patient's husband who was eavesdropping at the door to Freud's therapy room. The realization came to Freud when he bade farewell to the woman patient with a "Goodbye, Sir," a Freudian slip to be sure.

Characteristic too of a small group is that the group is small enough so that every member has the opportunity to participate. With the addition of each new member participation opportunities decrease. This is why the upper limit for a small group is set at nine. When group size exceeds this number the group tends to break into smaller groups, i.e., little side discussions begin and a single group focus becomes tenuous. Moreover, the group tends to take on the characteristics of public communication.

In *public communication* there is usually one speaker and a group of listeners. A student giving a speech in a public speaking class is engaging in public communication. Other examples would be a citizen addressing a town hall meeting or a politician giving a stock stump speech. In public communication the interaction among participants is dramatically reduced in comparison with small group communication. Aside from a question and answer session at the end of the presentation, the audience, for the most part, is passive.

Even less real-time interaction is afforded the audience in *mass communication*. In mass communication one communication agent sends a message to a mass audience which has no opportunity to interact with the sending agent in real time. Mass communication messages are mediated electronically or by print and many of these mediated messages are prepared well in advance of the presentation. Examples of such communication are newspapers, magazines, TV shows, etc. In these cases interaction with audience members in real-time is virtually impossible. For these reasons mass communication audiences, particularly TV audiences, have been described as passive, i.e., non-interactive.

It can be seen from the above that the small group allows certain interaction dynamics to occur that do not occur at the interpersonal level. And it is at the small group level that maximum opportunities for participation among group members can occur. When the number of participants exceeds nine those opportunities decrease and the group can then take on the appearance of a collection of smaller subgroups or a public communication situation.

The Group Versus the Individual

Two heads are better than one.
Too many cooks spoil the broth.

Is a group superior to an individual? For some things at least the answer seems to be obvious, particularly if the task is a physical one. To carry a piano to a third-floor walk-up apartment is not a solitary task. Much help is needed. For non-physical tasks, the research finds generally that a group is superior to an individual in solving problems, making decisions, and completing tasks. For example, Lumsden and Lumsden, (2000, p. 9) note that research going back more than 50 years has documented how effective groups can be. The same authors cite one study which found that groups outperformed their best member 97% of the time. And Beebe and Masterson (2000, p. 11) ask, "Why are groups and teams such an often-used method of getting results? Because most of the time, groups do achieve higher quality results than do individuals working alone."

The apparent superiority of the group over the individual may be the result of a number of factors. In groups there is a pooling of information; this is particularly true of teams where members are selected on the basis of their having different but complementary skills. In solving a problem, an individual may tend to go down a "blind alley" and not know it; in a group at least one member is likely to check such an errant excursion. Groups can stimulate. Members can stimulate one another and there are times when the group gets "on a roll." These are exciting and very often creative times.

At the same time, groups are not always superior. Groups can become dysfunctional and nonproductive. Dysfunctionality can be a result of inter-personal animosities, lack of organizational support for the group and its mission, dominance of a single member, and members' animosity toward the group because they have to serve on it, for example. Moreover, the individual has been found to be superior to the group when the decision to be made must be made immediately or when the task is either very simple or very complex. In emergency situations, disasters, surgeries, and on the battlefield, for instance, decisions must be made immediately. There is no time for a meeting. Simple tasks like making photocopies also require no meetings. Complex tasks often are put in the domain of an individual because that individual is the only one competent enough to deal with the task. Here Einstein is often cited as an example. How many groups meeting for how long would come up with the Theory of Relativity?

Looking at the final score, therefore, in the duel between the group and the individual we can say that, on balance, the group has won. The group is generally superior to the individual in task performance, decision making, and problem solving. It is for this reason that the majority of decisions that affect our lives are made by groups.

The Importance of Studying Small Group and Team Communication

It is important to study small group and team communication because of the pervasiveness of groups and the consequences of their actions, because virtually everyone is or will be a group participant, and because groups are important in the establishment and maintenance of self-concept.

As noted in the previous section, group actions are generally superior to individual actions and for this reason groups are used pervasively. As a consequence, everyone's life is directed and monitored by group decisions. Think, for example, of the control exercised by the committees, the subcommittees, the caucuses, etc., that advise lawmakers on legislative issues. These legislative groups have a tremendous influence on our lives and, of course, the government is only one agency in a web of agencies where groups are making decisions affecting our lives. Given this incredible influence of group actions on our lives it behooves us to understand the small group and team communication phenomena.

While group actions have a tremendous effect on the individual, most individuals are or will be members of task groups and teams, thereby shouldering the responsibility for the decisions that affect others. Here again it is important that the individual understand the workings of the group. Participation is not enough; if it were, every participant would be an expert. Thorough understanding and expertise are not attained simply through participation, but rather through study of group phenomena as well.

Finally, it is important to study small group and team communication because communication in this setting serves in the acquisition and maintenance of self-concept. There is a tendency to see group activity as purely task activity and devoid of psychodynamics. This is not the case though for, in group participation, group members receive feedback that tells them who they are; how valuable, cherished, and competent they are; and what role has been made available for them to fill.

The sociologist, Erving Goffman (1959), has said, "Doing is being," meaning that one's being or sense of self is determined by what one does. Serving in a group is "doing" and such service, therefore, contributes to one's "being" or sense of self. A person who loses his job, for example, because of downsizing, mergers, takeovers, and so on, is understandably devastated by the loss. First, of course, is the loss of income, but sometimes almost equally devastating is the attendant loss of self. The person has no answer to the question, "What do you do?" Friends and family groups provide critical feedback that helps to sustain a positive self-concept, but for most adults this is not enough. We want to feel valuable in "outside" groups, outside our friends and family. The premiere outside group is the employment group. No group member is a robotic task worker, but instead, is a worker with socio-emotional and psychological needs. The study of small group and team communication will help, therefore, in the understanding and the satisfaction of these needs.

Addressing this same point, Erikson (1963) proposed a model of development from birth to death. Erikson's model is relevant to groups and self-concept because at each stage of development, Erikson says, there is an individual or group that has a significant impact on development and self-concept. Erikson's eight stages and the respective significant individual or group follows.

1. *Birth through First Year:* The Mother is the Significant Person.

2. *Through Second Year:* The Father is the Significant Person.

3. *Third Year through Fifth Year:* The Family is the Significant Group.

4. *The Sixth Year till the Onset of Puberty:* The Neighbor and School provide Significant-Other Groups.

5. *Adolescence:* Peer Groups become significant.

6. *Early Adulthood:* Friends, Intimates, and Workmates are the Significant Others.

7. *Middle Adulthood:* The Shared Household provides the Significant-Other Core.

8. *Late Adulthood:* Family is important but people often see humanity as being significant as they like to come to the conclusion that their lives have made a difference.

Noted in Erikson's model is a significant other or a group of significant others for each developmental stage. In the beginning of life significant others are the parents and the basic family. Next the radius of significant others expands to include schoolmates and neighbors; and with adolescence, peer groups take center stage. Later, partners and workmates enter the radius. And, at the end of life, significant others may include relatives, friends, and perhaps personal care workers, but also humanity in general. We want to think about what our life meant and whether we made a difference.

Paradoxes

In the study of small groups and teams there are at least two paradoxes that will continually be revealed. The first was stated by Robert Bales, a pioneer and prolific researcher in the field. Bales said:

> When attention is given to the task, strains are created in the social and emotional relations of the members of the group, and attention then turns to the solution of these problems. So long as the group devotes its activity simply to social emotional activity, however, the task is not getting done, and attention would be expected to turn again to the task areas (Bales, 1950, p. 8).

The quotation from Bales relates, of course, to the content of the previous section. Bales notes that although the group focuses on its task, the group will falter if its members' socio-emotional needs are not satisfied. On the other side of the coin, the group will suffer as well if too much attention is paid to those needs; the task will not be accomplished. A balance between task and socio-emotional needs is crucial if the group is to succeed.

The second paradox relates to individual freedom. We have a need for group affiliation. In the group, social needs are satisfied, most notably the need for maintenance of self-concept. At the same time, when we join a group we lose individual freedom because we eventually adopt the values of the group and identify with the group. Often, this is the reason for the anger and hostility expressed or suppressed by group members. They want to be in the group but they don't want to be in the group. Goffman described this paradox when he said, "To have a self one must fill a role, but to fill a role is to lose self." For example, a person marries and starts a family. Once having entered this group (the family) the person has new roles to fill, roles defined by society, culture, religion, immediate family, and spouse's family. Past freedoms and persona are gone. The new roles redefine the person's self and to violate the rules of the new roles is to invite negative consequences.

Summary

In this chapter basic definitions important to the study of small group and team communication were provided, the context of small group and team communication was discussed, group performance was compared and contrasted with individual performance, the importance of studying small group and team communication was examined, and two paradoxes that we face when we participate in small group and team communication were presented and discussed.

CHAPTER 2

GROUP CATEGORIES
AND TYPES

Dichotomous Categories

Groups can be placed in a number of dichotomous, i.e., either one or the other, categories: primary versus secondary, formal versus informal, task versus social, therapeutic versus non-therapeutic.

Primary Groups versus Secondary Groups

Primary groups are those in which the relationships among members are closest and the relationships are long lasting. Family and friend groups are primary groups. Characteristically there is a great deal of mutual disclosure and spontaneity among family and friends. In addition these primary group relationships often last for a lifetime. This is particularly true of family relations.

Secondary groups are those groups beyond family and close friends. Most individuals belong to many more primary groups than secondary groups. Examples of secondary groups are work groups, recreation groups, learning groups, workout groups, religious groups, and therapy groups. In secondary groups there is less self-disclosure and spontaneity than in primary groups. Instead, communication is more strategic or planned. At times secondary groups can become primary. Often when this happens it is a shared emotional experience that binds the members into a primary relationship. For example, soldiers who share the emotional experience of battle may form a close bond that lasts for the remainder of their days.

Formal versus Informal Groups

A *formal group* operates under the direction of an overt set of rules while an informal group is directed by an unwritten, covert set of rules. In large legislative groups interaction is formally directed by parliamentary procedures; "The honorable member from Delaware yields to the honorable member from Arizona," for example. In small groups, the most common set of formal overt rules is Robert's Rules of Order (Robert et al. 1990). The creator of Robert's Rules of Order, Colonel Henry Robert, derived the rules from British Parliamentary Procedures and related rules Thomas Jefferson established for the U.S. Senate. The rules can be seen as a kind of traffic control for group interaction. When strictly enforced the rules dictate who will talk and when, what topic can be discussed, and when, when discussion or debate can be interrupted or ended, and when a vote on a motion is to be taken.

It is often said that the rules of an *informal group* are written nowhere, taught by no one, but known implicitly by all. Most groups are informal, but emphasis must be placed on the fact that these groups still have rules, rules that are sometimes quite elaborate. Often the rules are difficult to state even though we know them. For example, if you were asked to state the rules of your family you could begin to construct the list but that list would be partial. How then are we to know the rules of an informal group? It would seem nonsensical to say that we follow a set of rules that we cannot recite. We usually know that a rule is a rule when someone violates it. Family rules that have been followed unwittingly for years often become manifest only when someone breaks the rule. Often it is a guest not familiar with the family's rules who is the transgressor. The longer the guest stays, the more family members discover the rules of the family. Why? Because they observe the guest breaking the rules. These violations can be tolerated for short periods of time but at some point someone must say, "In our home we do it this way."

Some groups do a formal-informal fade-in and fade-out. In some small groups, say a committee, the decision will be made to use Robert's Rules of Order. After several meetings, however, the group members become friendly and gradually abandon their adherence to Robert's Rules. But when the group is divided in its reaction to some critical issue, for example, the Chair may reinstate the rules: "Bob, we can't discuss that until it's put in the form of a motion and the motion is seconded." Now Bob is a bit shocked, because in just the last meeting anyone could speak at any time. Indeed, if Bob does put his concern in a motion and no one seconds it, he is "dead in the water;" his issue will not be discussed. Episodic returns to formality are usually not wise. Members often see such maneuvers as manipulative.

Sometimes hybrid groups form, part formal and part informal. For example, in an informal discussion group the following rule might be instated: "In this group no one can introduce a problem unless one also proposes a solution for that problem."

Task versus Social Groups

A *task group* convenes and labors for the purpose of accomplishing a task or achieving a goal. For example, a task group is formed to raise money for flood victims, a jury is formed to judge the accused, an appeals board exists to hear the appeal of aggrieved citizens, work groups meet routinely to finish their assigned tasks, and teams are staffed to do an assigned task and are then disbanded.

Social groups are formed and joined so that members can have fun, socialize, avoid loneliness, and so on. Virtually no production quotas or task-completion deadlines are given to social group members: we do not say, "Tonight everyone must complete ten units of fun."

When groups are formed they are, on the surface, known to be task or social groups, informing new members of what they may expect in the group. But as noted in Chapter 1, Bales pointed out that a pure task group is probably impossible. To keep a group attentive, the members' socio-emotional needs must be addressed. For this reason, there are Friday afternoon beer busts, company-sponsored sporting events, Caribbean cruises for quota breakers, and so on. The old aphorism, "All work and no play," has some merit.

In social groups members are satisfying their socio-emotional needs and are not seen as having to take time to also satisfy task needs. Satisfaction implies socio-emotional factors. Nonetheless, here again there seems to be some support for the "all play and no work" aphorism, suggested by the fact that social clubs and organizations, Kiwanis, Rotary, and Lions, for example, become service clubs. They give themselves tasks to complete.

Therapeutic and Non-therapeutic Groups

The basic criterion for entry into a therapeutic group is personal suffering which leads the sufferer to voluntarily enter a therapy group. There is also the avenue of involuntary entry which occurs when some legal edict dictates entry into a group.

Four of the basic defining characteristics of a therapeutic group follow.

- First, the group is led by a professionally-trained therapist, certified by a professional association and licensed to practice.

- Second, the rules of everyday social interaction are suspended or replaced. For example, in a therapeutic group, members might cry, shout, insult, confess, disclose very personal information, and speak for long periods of time. These are communicative behaviors that would not be tolerated in everyday discourse for any length of time.

- Third, the therapist believes that there is something in the group experience that is therapeutic. For instance, if a group is composed of newly-divorced individuals the therapist may feel that identification is important, i.e., that it is good for each member to be with and identify with others who have had the same recent experience and who are suffering. On the other hand a different therapist might believe that the newly divorced person who is suffering should not be placed in a group with other newly-divorced persons. Instead, the person should be placed in a group of divorced individuals who have successfully coped with the suffering and trauma of a divorce. The therapist here is hoping that the one newly-divorced person in the group will have role models to provide help and guidance on the way to recovery.

- A fourth and final defining characteristic of a therapeutic group is that it provides socio-emotional support for its members, who may feel lonely and isolated physically and/or psychologically.

There is a large number of therapies that are designed for or that can be adapted for groups. Herink (1980) says that the actual number is unknown. In preparing to edit *The Psychotherapy Handbook*, Herink first identified 350 psychotherapeutic systems and techniques. This list was then reduced to 250 for publication in the handbook. Of the 250 therapies, 16 were specifically designed for the small group environment although many more of the others were adaptable to the group environment. The numbers show that the psychotherapeutic enterprise is vast in scope and is one that uses the group experience to facilitate recovery.

Non-therapeutic groups are defined by default, i.e., all groups that are not therapeutic. It could be argued that there is some therapeutic value to almost all groups, particularly social groups. The sheer presence of others who can contribute to satisfying socio-emotional needs indeed can be therapeutic. The therapeutic value here, however, serves to maintain members' feelings of adequacy and self-worth as a by-product of the inter-action. It is probably not the primary reason for joining the group.

Specific Types of Groups

Above we listed general categories into which specific groups can be placed. In this section we will discuss a number of specific groups.

The Family

The family is a primary group. It is a group for which we all have a "membership card" and it is the group that we cannot quit. Even though we may physically separate ourselves from family members we cannot do so psychologically. Even after a family member's death, the memory remains. The psychiatrist, Eric Berne, often said that we will hear our parents' voices in our heads long after they have died. A line from a Neil Diamond song makes this manifest: *If I close my eyes I can hear my mother saying, "Neil, it's time for supper."* Because the family is a primary group, communication in the family is spontaneous. Feelings are expressed with little or no editing. The feelings can range from anger, hatred, jealousy to love, affection, and sharing. These feelings can lead to aggressive or competitive behaviors or to supportive or cooperative behaviors. It is often said that people would never treat strangers in the same negative ways they sometimes treat family members. And at the same time these same people will rally to the support of family members in times of threat or crisis, giving validity to the aphorism, "Blood is thicker than water." So burdened is the family experience with emotion that it is not surprising that the trip to the therapist for most individuals is prompted by a family problem or a problem that can be traced to family relationships.

Contributing to the emotionality of the family group is the close physical proximity in which family members live. There are almost no secrets and the behavior of any one family member can be exposed for all other members to scrutinize.

Adolescent Groups

Between childhood and maturity is a developmental period called adolescence. If you are a parent of an adolescent you may have the scars, for this is the period of rebellion. If you just emerged from this period, you know the grief you might have caused your parents and family. Adolescents want to be independent of their parents; parental influence weakens. What matters most, of course, are the adolescent's friends. Adolescents encapsulate themselves in an almost impenetrable membrane. Within their capsules they listen to music, exchange endless phone calls and emails, cruise the malls, and invent new activities and jargon. There are emotional highs and lows, earning the adolescent the common description, "hormones with feet." During this period, of course, the adolescent reaches puberty and there are indeed marked hormonal changes.

What are the purposes of adolescent groups? They have no tasks to complete, no goals to reach or quotas to meet. It is just dating, dancing, and hanging out, and when members are not together physically they stay in touch with endless phone calls and emails. On the surface there seems to be no purpose, but, in fact, such adolescent groups serve important purposes that have to do with identity and social competence.

Every day we are faced with the same question, "Who am I?" For the child that question is answered by parents and other family members who respond to the child's presence, deeds, and words with a range of responses on the favorable-unfavorable continuum. This feedback serves to establish the child's identity and self-concept; the child sees himself or herself as one who is worthy, competent, and so on because of this feedback. With entrance into adolescence, however, parental feedback is not enough and, at times, is resented. The adolescent seeks approval from peers and, thus, identity is now shaped and maintained by the adolescent group. The adolescent must first be accepted into an adolescent group and thereafter must conform to its norms in order to receive positive feedback which contributes to identity formation. The identity provided by the adolescent's peer group is, in part, a new identity; it is not necessarily the identity acquired as a child and, thus, the new identity represents independence. Adolescents often communicate their new identities through dress, hair styles, tattoos, piercings, and slang, for example. At times, the messages are quite blatantly designed specifically, it seems, to shock mom, dad, granny, and the whole gang. The messages are screaming, "Look at me," not necessarily with approval, since the peer group provides the approval, but just give me attention.

Social competencies are learned in adolescent groups. Learning to meet and get along with new people; learning to resolve conflicts and resolve problems with peers when there are no parental figures to order and direct; learning to persuade others, to have them go along with your suggestions and to adopt your points of view; and learning to make yourself attractive to others so that you might be considered an ideal dating partner are just some of the social competencies learned in adolescence. Inclusion in the group is not enough. The adolescent must bring to the group something that is empowering. For example, the adolescent might be liked by fellow group members because of a sense of humor, money and material possessions, athletic talent, musical talent, physical attractiveness, and so on. These attributes empower the adolescent, for to have one or more of the valued attributes means that the adolescent has the social currency with which to bargain. The bargaining is seldom overt. The adolescent humorist does not say, "I'll tell only two jokes if you don't buy lunch." It is much more subtle than that. Learning to engage in social bargaining is also a key social competence.

Work Groups

Before the industrial revolution, most people worked on farms and the work group was the family. And with little mechanization on the farm a large family was desirable. Non-farm work groups, for the most part, were also families. Bakers, butchers, smiths, shopkeepers, and millers had their shops and mills in their homes or nearby. Of course in pre-industrial times most people worked on farms.

With the advent of the industrial age work groups became centralized and large. The smith's little shop under the spreading chestnut tree became a behemoth industrial complex, the River Rouge complex of the Ford Motor Company, or the over 100 miles of mines and mills of the U.S. and J & L Steel corporations strung along the Allegheny, Monongahela, and Ohio Rivers in Pittsburgh, for example. Thousands of workers streamed through the gates of these complexes to work each of the three daily shifts. The workers were seen literally as cogs in the machine, replaceable parts, as replaceable as gear, shaft, press, drop forge, cable, chain or belt. Communication was top down and communication among workers was discouraged. Workers' group affiliations were with family and ethnic organizations. To this day in the old mine and mill towns are buildings with signs of those organizations, the Russian Club, the Ukrainian Club, Croatian Hall, Sons of Italy and the Polish Falcons, for example.

Now the industrial age has given way to the information age. In the information age material assets, mines and mills, for instance, are less important. Instead, ideas and the people who have them and generate them are important. And ideas are generated in small groups and teams. So the wheel has turned a full 360 degrees. Before the industrial age, work groups were small and now in the information age they are once again small.

The present and future work group will be fluid and ever-changing. Job stability will not exist. Conlin (2000, p. 170) recently reported, "A typical 32-year-old, for example, has already held nine jobs according to the Labor Department. Experts predict that these same workers will have as many as 20 different positions in their lifetimes." And Peters (2000, p. 172) adds that "in the next few years, whether at a tiny company or behemoth, we will be working with an eclectic mix of contract teammates from around the globe, many of whom we will never meet face-to-face. Every project will call for a new team, composed of specially tailored skills. Information that is more than hours old will be viewed with concern."

Work groups are task groups and thus they are formed to achieve a goal. A work group is needed because one person cannot do the task alone or because a variety of skills is needed, all of which are not possessed by a single individual. But, as mentioned in Chapter 1, there is another aspect of the work group: the feedback from fellow workers serves to maintain self-concept, to validate you as a competent and worthy person. In the fluid and ever-changing environment of the information age it will be more difficult to secure this necessary feedback. If workers become floating agents selling their services globally on a worker E-bay-type auction site, the chances for camaraderie are highly diminished. The new information worker may have to find the necessary validating feedback in other group venues, family, friends, clubs, and so on. Already many workers who have been sent home to work report missing the camaraderie of fellow workers, the hallway hellos, the lunches, and the little bits of gossip.

A final note on work groups and teams concerns their management. Traditionally teams have been managed, often in business at least, by a chief operating officer. But the COO's days may be numbered. Brady (2000, p. 125) says, "What killed the COO? The job became a victim of employment empowerment." And, "Increasingly corporate complexity and the shift to team management are killing the chief operating officer." So teams are no longer just subservient task groups but now management task groups as well.

Self-Help Groups

Whatever the disease, condition or addiction, invariably a self-help group is created to provide mutual support for members and to help its members find relief from the disease, condition or addiction they have in common. The focus in such a group may be a physical pathology, for instance, cancer, heart disease, spinal cord injury; behavioral control, psychopathology, alcoholism, drug addiction, gambling addiction; or a social condition, for example, feelings of isolation, alienation, or discrimination because of age, gender, race, marital status, social class, or ethnicity.

The self-help group is member controlled. It is, therefore, said to be quasi-therapeutic meaning that it is not a full-fledged therapeutic endeavor. It is not led by a professional therapist, one who is certified by a recognized professional association, who is licensed to practice in a given state or province, and who is directed by a code of ethics. The absence of a professional therapist in the self-help group is a source of tension between professionals and self-help groups. Many times professionals feel that self-help groups are well-intentioned but not necessarily competent to deal with their problems. Just having a problem does not make us experts in the problem area. Professionals might argue that having cancer does not make us oncologists, that having a baby does not make us obstetricians, and that being an alcoholic does not make us behavior modification specialists. The professionals are saying that to remove those problems or at least to lessen their effects requires training, training in a research-based curriculum and clinical training with actual patients or clients. There must also be a professional code of conduct, a code whose first line was written by Hippocrates: "First above all else do no harm." Codes of conduct or ethical codes recognize that professional therapists are in a privileged and powerful position. Because of this there must be strict guidelines to prevent therapists from using their privilege and power to exploit patients and clients who are suffering, and who, therefore, may be vulnerable.

Self-help group members reject the arguments made by the professional therapists with the response, "Thank you, but we will do it ourselves." The emotionality of this response varies. Some self-help groups take a very cynical view of the professional and see the professional as a pretentious, condescending, know-it-all with a fancy vocabulary who is probably only conducting therapy sessions in order to write another book. This, of course, is an extreme and minority position. The main reason self-help groups exclude the professional has to do with the key dynamic of self-help groups and that dynamic is *identification.* To identify with others is to show that you are one of them. A self-help group member feels that unless you experience the disease, condition, or addiction, you cannot know how I feel. In short, you cannot identify with me, you simply will not be able to understand my suffering. Words can only go so far to explain a person's suffering. After that only mutual experience can lead to understanding and mutual experience underlies the identification process.

For example, if you are a member of a family where one member is an alcoholic, you can tell about all the birthday and holiday parties that were ruined, you can recite a litany of broken promises and disappointments, you can tell of family money misspent, you can tell of cover-up stories you had to create, you can talk about hangovers, and filthy and smelly messes, and you can tell of verbal and physical abuse. You can tell all these things to other people, but if they have not experienced it, they will not fully understand. In like manner, the veteran suffering from post-traumatic stress syndrome (PTSS) simply can try to explain to the non-combat-experienced the flashbacks and nightmares of incoming rockets, mortars, and machine gun fire; of poisonous snakes, spiders, and lizards; of seeing friends have their throats cut, being maimed, burned, or literally being blown to bits; and of killing others with guns, rockets, or in hand-to-hand combat with bayonets and knives. The shouts and screams of the wounded and dying and the smell of ammo powder, and the look of death simply will not go away. But the listener cannot truly comprehend.

There are times of rapprochement between professionals and self-help groups. For example, Alcoholics Anonymous, the pioneer, longest-running, and most geographically-penetrating self-help group has been cooperating with professionals in the treatment of acute alcoholism. A person suffering from acute alcoholism is first admitted to an acute-care hospital for detoxification and is treated by medical personnel. Next the person is sent to a chemical-abuse rehabilitation center for 30 to 60 days to be treated by a variety of psychotherapists. Following this, the person joins AA and is encouraged to regularly attend meetings.

Growth Groups

A *growth group* is designed to help participants realize their full potential in life. This realization comes about through the group experience. At the heart of growth groups are changes in *perception*, perception of self, of others, of the world and of what can be in the world. How do you begin to think about perception? One way is to consider what an old philosopher suggested. Stand on a chair and look at your room. You see a different room.

Growth group theory assumes that there is a much more capable, competent, and more socially-attractive and socially-adept and more authentic you than you know about. And although you live in a world that you think you know, there are whole other worlds made invisible to you because of narrow perceptions.

Operationally, therefore, the task of a growth group leader is to devise techniques to alter perceptions.

One common strategy for changing perceptions is to move people from *emotional zero* in either a positive or negative direction. On the positive side are emotions like love, affection, happiness, and pleasure; on the negative side, fear, anger, hostility, and disgust. The ancient Greeks were not unaware of this and knew the importance of the pathos factor in persuasion. *Pathos* means "feeling" and an approach to persuading an audience is the emotional appeal, an appeal designed to arouse the audience's feelings and emotions. And, of course, if persuasion is successful, the audience will have new perceptions.

Deprivation is a second strategy for changing perceptions. Studies have shown that deprivation of sleep, food, water, bathroom privileges, and physical confinement, for instance, lead to perceptual changes and emotional arousal. Sleep deprivation is particularly interesting. Have you ever stayed awake for three days? If you have, you surely experienced perceptual changes. Common objects in your environment probably appeared distorted. Moving stimuli, say pigeons in your path, may have looked like monsters. In fact, long-term sleep deprivation can cause hallucinogenic-type reactions. We begin to lose our grip; the old perceptual world is destabilized. In fact, Aldous Huxley, (author of the *Doors of Perception)* would often say in his speeches that extended sleep deprivation can produce effects that mimic the effects of naturally occurring hallucinogenic drugs, peyote, for example. Food and water deprivation are also arousing. And if we are deprived of bathroom privileges, we are aroused not only by physiologic distress but also by shame at the thought of having an "accident."

Another strategy for changing perceptions is to create an environment in which an individual discloses or reveals personal secrets. The general tendency for all of us is to become emotional when we do reveal, confess, and tell our secrets. In such a state, too, our old perceptions are destabilized and we are open to new perceptions and possible growth.

Three examples of growth groups are T-Groups, Marathon Encounter Groups, and EST.

T-Groups

T-Groups (Golembiewski and Miller, 1980) constitute a set of experiential, educational designs for understanding the self in relation to others with the small group membership providing both the context for learning and crucial feedback and emotional support for the learners. T-Group procedures were developed at the National Training Laboratory in Bethel, Maine in 1947. Growth for an individual in a T-Group emerges in a three-step process:

1. Unfreezing: Here the individual in the T-Group is provided with a supportive environment that allows open expression of things thought but never said and of actions contemplated but never carried out. The threats always felt to be associated with discussing these things are reduced or eliminated. In the words of a poet, "Speech after long silence, it is right."

2. Testing: Here new ideas and perceptions about self, others, and the world are tested in the safe environment of the T-Group.

3. Re-Freezing: Here new ideas and perceptions are integrated into an individual's attitudinal or belief repertoire. Thus, here is where the growth occurs.

Support and relief experienced in the safe environment of the group generates the emotion needed to facilitate emergence of new perceptions. Metaphorically, the group becomes the safe harbor for the lost sailor who experiences strong feelings of fear when lost at sea and then sheds tears of joy when rescued and brought to LeHarve de Grace.

Think of the burdens that you carry on your mind, the fear, the guilt, the anxiety, the worry, and the anger that negatively affect your relationships with others and your general performance. Now imagine yourself finding a small group of supporting and trusting people with whom you might share your burdens, talk about them, and, as a result, gain new perceptions that might allow you to restructure your thoughts and actions for the better. If this were to happen, then indeed you would have grown.

Marathon Encounter Groups

A *Marathon Encounter Group* (Bach, 1980) is a group where there is an intensification and acceleration of genuine encounter through a deliberate instigation of group pressure focused on behavior change. This is facilitated by a time-extended schedule requiring uninterrupted sessions lasting from 16 to over 40 hours. As you can probably imagine, when a group is confined to a given space for long periods of time, group pressure begins to arouse the emotions. The polite, gracious, game-playing, phony behaviors that participants exhibit at the beginning of the marathon session begin to give way to more honest and authentic behaviors that often are less gracious. Participants begin to "level" with one another. It is truth-telling time. Conflict often emerges and emotions are high. Participants are asked how they feel at the moment and are told how their feelings contradict their actions. The accusatory word, "phony," is thrown around with great frequency. For example, if participant John says he never plays games, shouts of "phony" undoubtedly fill the air. John's assertion stands in contradiction to the other participants' perception of him. John must now work on this contradiction and perhaps come to realize that his assertion was in conflict even with his own feelings. Out of such realizations growth is said to occur and hopefully a new, more honest and authentic John can reenter the world.

EST (Erhard Seminars Training)

Erhard Seminars Training (EST) (Smith, 1975) was named for its founder, Werner Erhard, a neonym scavenged from the names of two famous Germans, Ludwig Erhard and Werner von Braun. In a typical EST session participants gather in a hotel, usually for a weekend. Before them is a Marine drill sergeant type who tells the participants that they may leave and receive a refund in the first ten minutes; after that they will do what they are told for the rest of the weekend; they will eat, drink, smoke, and go to the bathroom only when told to do so. "At least if you don't let them pee you begin to get their attention," according to Erhard. They are told they might have to remain in their chairs for 12 to 18 hours. The "sergeant" then begins to berate the participants with scatological insults. Some participants try to respond and the "sergeant" responds with biting insults. Emotions begin to run high, provoked by extended confinement, hunger, and thirst, the need for a cigarette, the need to use the bathroom, and the apparently absolutely meaningless and absurd proceedings. With the atmosphere so emotionally charged, participants begin to say things they would not ordinarily say in public: "dirty" words, taboo thoughts, and so on. They attack the "sergeant," the proceedings, and, in general, begin to rebel. Someone will invariably shout, "This is a bunch of crap!!" The "sergeant" appears pleased and he may say, for example, "Now you are beginning to get it!" What's going on? Well, the seminar is a metaphor for life and if the participants say, "This (seminar) is a bunch of crap," they are really on their way to concluding that much of life itself is a bunch of crap. This is really "getting it." And just as the participants began not to care a whit about the seminar and what they said in it, they will, in kind, begin to take the same attitude toward many aspects of their own lives. This is growth in EST.

EST peaked in the seventies but has had somewhat of a rebirth in the new century under a new name, the Landmark Forum or Forum for short (Grigoriadis, 2001). The Forum promises personal fulfillment through a grueling three-day program. Its parentage, EST, is unmistakable.

Concluding Remarks on Growth Groups

Growth groups were popular in the 60s, 70s, and 80s, but aside from the apparent EST revival their popularity has waned. It may be that they were a cyclical phenomenon and they had their season, or that all the interested consumers have been satisfied, or most likely, that it is difficult or impossible to be totally authentic or totally honest in everyday life. The social order may need to be maintained by some healthy doses of flattery and insincerity.

Summary

In this chapter the small group catalog was opened in order that group categories and types could be examined. First a number of dichotomous group categories were presented and discussed. Included were primary and secondary groups, formal and informal groups, task and social groups, and therapeutic and non-therapeutic groups. Second, a number of specific types of groups were presented and discussed. Included here were the family, the adolescent group, the work group, the self-help group, and growth groups.

CHAPTER 3

COMMUNICATION IN GROUPS
THEORETICAL CONSIDERATIONS

Virtually everyone has some notion of theory. A high profile crime is committed in your neighborhood. The crime is unsolved. In such a situation people can be heard to say, "Well, my theory is...." President Kennedy was assassinated almost 40 years ago and still today people talk about the one-gunman theory and the multi-gunman theory. In each of these cases there is one correct notion of theory and that notion is mystery.

In this chapter, theories and models of small group communication are presented.

A *theory* is a set of systematically interrelated hypotheses, premises, assumptions, facts, and observations pertaining to a particular phenomenon.

A *model* is a representation of a thing, process, or phenomenon. Often the distinction between theories and models blurs and some writers use the two terms interchangeably.

In this text, the model is distinguished by its representational nature. Theories on the other hand, are considered to be more comprehensive and to be more concerned with the "wh" questions: who?, what?, why?, where?, and when?, and the how? question. Frequently a theory contains, explicitly or implicitly, a model. The model serves as the capstone for the theoretical structure.

Why do people construct theories? The primary purpose is to *organize,* or systematically interrelate, the hypotheses, premises, assumptions, facts, and observations pertaining to a phenomenon. Think of your own experiences where you have been in a quandary. Quite possibly you felt a need to organize, to pull things together. In like manner, individuals who study small group relations feel a need to organize what they know about small group phenomena.

Theories, secondly, enable us to *explain* phenomena. The wh and how questions enter in here. As any parent knows, there comes a time when the child is obsessed with asking why questions. Adults too have similar inquisitive impulses. Query individuals about a crime, a freak occurrence in nature, or a political maneuver, and they will often reply, "Well, my theory is …." And, in a sense, the individuals are theorists because they are organizing and explaining.

Third, theories enable us to *predict.* Having organized hypotheses, premises, assumptions, facts, and observations about a phenomenon and having explained a phenomenon, places us in a better position for predicting future events. Theories subsequently presented will suggest reasons for small group relationships being sustained or terminated. Awareness of these reasons allows us to predict the course of events in the future.

Fourth, theories are said to be *heuristic,* that is, they serve to raise new questions and generate new hypotheses for testing. When a theory is formulated, the consequent response is, "If this new theory is true, then X, Y,

Z and so on must also be true." Of course, the verification of X, Y, and Z requires further research and study.

Finally, all theories contain some *mystery.* There are premises, assumptions, and hypotheses not verified but used, nonetheless, in the construction of a theory. We talked above about the mystery surrounding the assassination of President Kennedy. Freud talked about the id, ego, and superego. No one, of course, has ever seen these conceptual "children" of Freud. The concepts are crucial to his theory in spite of their amorphic qualities. Theories totally verified or refuted are no longer theories but facts.

Theories are often referred to as "points of view." The reason for this reference is that, while all the theorists can view the same phenomena, diverse interpretational emphases are manifest. Diversity in interpretation can be seen in Freud's statement that at times a cigar is just a cigar. Here Freud was telling his audience to refrain from forever attaching extended meanings to everything, a practice which, of course, Freud, himself spawned. Theories of small group and team communication will vary, therefore, not on the behavioral level, but on the interpretive level. Different theories will have different points of view.

A closing comment on theories has to do with the connotations attached to the word, "theory." For many, theory connotes complexity, etherealness, not in the real world, and so on. For those who have these negative connotations, recall that everyone theorizes to one degree or another. Theorizing is not an activity given exclusively to anyone or any group. And if "theory" remains aversive, try thinking of "theory" as a point of view or an approach.

And last, when studying the theories in this chapter, look constantly for commonalities among theories. At times a particular concept will surface in one or more theories.

In this chapter we will look at a number of theoretical perspectives on communication in the small group and team. With each perspective one theorist will be highlighted. We will see what recommendations each theorist has for communication. We will notice that no theorist satisfies all the requirements of theory as they were outlined in the definition and discussion above. There are two reasons to account for this. First, few theories in the human behavior field are rigorously constructed. Often theories develop out of a hunch, a notion, or a metaphor. Second, the theories as presented here are necessarily abbreviated. Each of the theorists has written one or more books on his or her theory. In one chapter we can only present thumbnail sketches of the theories and, then, after the roster has been presented, we will critically evaluate these theories.

Theories of Small Group and Team Communication

Berne's Transactional Theory

The genesis for Eric Berne's Transactional Theory (Berne, 1967) was a classical child psychology study by Rene Spitz. Spitz found that institutionalized babies were dying at an unexpectedly high rate in spite of good nutrition and hygiene, and in the absence of disease-causing agents. Investigation showed that the babies were not hugged, cuddled, rocked, or stroked, but when these tactile behaviors were instated the babies began to thrive.

From the Spitz study, Berne took his motto, "If you are not stroked, you will shrivel up and die" as indeed did the babies in Spitz's study. Berne noted that this is true not only for babies, but also for adults. For adults, though, the strokes are not so much physical as verbal. Thus it appears that the motive for much communication is to obtain strokes. A *stroke* is a recognition of one person by another. It can be as simple as a "Hi," a multi-word response, or the receiving of the Nobel Prize. An exchange of strokes is a *transaction,* thus the theory's name, Transactional Analysis.

There are four types of verbal interactions whereby we may obtain strokes: rituals, pastimes, games, and true intimacy.

A *ritual* is an exchange of strokes that is repeated day after day and from which no new information emerges. An example of a ritual is the Hi-Hi exchange between people at the beginning of each group meeting. It can be more elaborate: "Hi, how are you?" "Fine, how are you?" Rituals may seem to be trivial and of no consequence but imagine if no one said "Hi" to you for a day or longer. You would begin to "shrivel up." You would be traumatized.

Pastimes are extended conversations from which new information may be forthcoming, where there are no hidden agendas, and where a climate of social acceptance remains. Morning elevator conversations about the weather are an example; so are "Remember when…." and "Have you ever been to…?"

A *game* is a series of transactions in which one participant has a hidden agenda and wants to gain something from someone else without the other's being aware of the motive. For example, a man suddenly befriends an elderly, rich widow who lives nearby and has no immediate family. The man mows the woman's lawn, picks up her mail, does her banking and so on. The widow says, "You are such a good neighbor" to which the man replies, "What are neighbors for?" The end move in the game, of course, is when the man takes the widow to his lawyer to have a new will written (the payoff) in which everything in the widow's estate is left to the man. The woman may or may not have ever known that she was the mark or victim of the game. And why do all of us at one time or another become the mark or victim in a game? Because games provide strokes and they bring about involvement, and involvement provokes emotional arousal, a state we often equate with meaningfulness.

In the state of *true intimacy* communicating parties are involved and aroused without playing games. Here there are no hidden agendas and we experience mutual joy.

Sometimes in a group, for example, for no identifiable reason, everyone begins to giggle and laugh and just can't stop; this can be considered a state of mutual joy, a state of true intimacy. True intimacy does not refer necessarily to a romantic state but it is a state that can occur between or among individuals.

In interactions, therefore, people obtain strokes in rituals, pastimes, games, and true intimacy, according to Berne. Berne also suggested the ways in which people communicate in these types of interactions with his PAC model. Berne said that anyone at any time can communicate through one of three modes: the Parent (P) mode characterized by commanding, warning, moralizing, judging, analyzing, and interrogating; the Adult (A) mode characterized by tenuousness, possibility, allowing the other person to save face, civility, and affability; and the Child (C) mode characterized by emotion, the positive emotions of joy and happiness, and the negative emotions of anger, rage, tantrums, and exhibitionism.

In task group situations we would expect group members to communicate primarily through the Adult mode. They might say things like "I think there may be possibilities here," or "In my opinion...," or, "There's one part of this proposal I don't understand," and so on. They would say these things rather than "Your idea stinks" or "That will never work." Such responses fall into Berne's Child mode category and would give reminders of a real child's, "My daddy is bigger than your daddy" and "I don't care," in response to a parental, "If you don't eat your spinach you won't be big and strong." At any time, any person can respond through any one of Berne's three communication modes: Parent, Adult, and Child.

Gordon's Effective Communication Theory

"Communicators," says Thomas Gordon, "are blamed but not trained." Gordon has written a number of communication books with "effectiveness" in the title (2000, 1986, 1974). Gordon talks about effective listening and effective talking. The effective listener may show effectiveness passively by just saying nothing or may demonstrate active listening by giving the speaker feedback which confirms that what the speaker said was heard. A common active listening technique is to echo or paraphrase what the speaker said. For example, if the speaker says, "I began working here two years age," the listener might reply, "Two years ago, eh."

On the talking side, Gordon lists a number of ineffective talking strategies. Included among them are:

- Directing and Commanding
- Warning, Admonishing, and Threatening
- Exhorting, Moralizing, and Preaching
- Advising and Giving Suggestions
- Lecturing and Giving Logical Arguments
- Judging, Criticizing, Disagreeing, and Blaming
- Global Praising
- Name Calling, Ridiculing, and Shaming
- Interpreting, Analyzing, and Diagnosing
- Reassuring and Counseling
- Probing, Questioning, and Interpreting
- Withdrawing, Distracting, and Diverting

One of Gordon's most basic rules for effective talking is to turn "you" messages into "I" messages. For example, in a group, instead of saying "Your idea is confusing," Gordon would recommend saying, "I'm having a little difficulty understanding this idea." And in like manner, instead of saying, "We tried your idea years ago and it didn't work," an effective talker might say, "I'm wondering if this idea has been tried before."

You might wonder what "the big deal" is about using the word, "you." The word, "you," points out and it is often taken as an accusation; it often "corners" the other person. "I" statements are less accusatory and allow the other person to save face as a result.

Dale Carnegie's Influence Theory

One of the most pervasive and enduring sets of suggestions for communicating is contained in Dale Carnegie's *How to Win Friends and Influence People* (1994, 1936). Although not presented as a theory, it, nonetheless, is built on a number of assumptions and premises concerning communication for effect. A summary of Carnegie's theory appears below.

Fundamental Techniques in Handling People

- Don't blame other people.
- People desire to be important, so make them feel important.
- Phrase things toward your audience's point of view.

Ways to Make People Like You

- Become genuinely interested in other people.
- Smile.
- Remember that a person's name is the sweetest and most important sound in the world.
- Be a good listener. Encourage others to talk about themselves.
- Talk in terms of the other person's interest.
- Make the other person feel important, and do it sincerely.

Ways to Win People to Your Way of Thinking

- The only way to get the best of an argument is to avoid it.
- Show respect for the other person's opinions.
- Never tell people that they are wrong.
- If you are wrong, admit it quickly and emphatically.
- Begin speaking in a friendly way. Get the other person saying "Yes" immediately.

- Let the other person do a great deal of the talking.
- Let the other people feel that the idea is theirs.
- Try honestly to see things from the other person's point of view.
- Be sympathetic with the other person's ideas and desires.
- Appeal to the nobler motives.
- Dramatize your ideas.
- Throw down a challenge to the other person.

Ways to Change People Without Giving Offense or Arousing Resentment

- If you must find fault, begin and end with praise.
- Call attention to people's mistakes indirectly.
- Talk about your own mistakes before criticizing the other person.
- Ask questions instead of giving direct orders.
- Let the other person save face.
- Praise the slightest improvement and praise every improvement. Be lavish in your praise.
- Give the person a fine reputation to live up to (i.e., suggest the appropriate behavior for the person to follow).
- Use encouragement.
- Make the fault you want to correct seem easy to correct.
- Make the other person happy about doing the thing you suggest.

What the above reveals is a saturation strategy of respect, praise, flattery to make the person to whom you are talking feel good, special, and competent, so competent indeed that that person is willing to change his or her mind. At the same time, the other person is allowed to save face and, as a result, does not feel defensive. Perhaps you have been in a group with people who are fresh from a Carnegie course. Often they are a bit gushy, "icky," and sugary. But, at the same time, there are few who can resist the charm, courtesy, and civility of the true "Carnegie-ite." We will talk later about the ethics of Carnegie's method.

Leary's Reflex Theory

Before he emerged as a celebrity in the drug-drenched 60s, the psyche-delic, LSD, hippie decade, Timothy Leary (Leary, 1953) was a researcher in human communication. One highlight of his research was a large research project on human communication. What Leary found was that a large percentage of communication behaviors are simply *reflexes* or auto-matic responses. Such behaviors are so automatic that they appear to be unconscious, and even quite different from the interactants' perceptions of the behaviors. It is important to remind ourselves of the nature of a reflex. Remember a time when your physician hit your kneecap with a rubber hammer. There was a resultant patellar reflex or "knee jerk." You did not think about moving your leg; the response was automatic. Leary believed that many interactional responses were independent of the cogni-tive processes that occur in an encounter as described by other theories. This is compatible with the reflex notion. Therefore, Leary's approach is quite distinct from the other theories presented in this text in that it is essentially concept free. Absent are the concepts of perception, cognition, balance, imbalance, and so on.

Leary listed sixteen interactional reflexes, giving the evoking stimuli and the reflexive responses. The 16 are listed below in Person A-Person B format.

1. If Person A manages, directs, or leads, then the reflexive response from Person B will be obedience.
2. If Person A acts confidently and takes independent actions, then the reflexive response from Person B will be inferiority.

3. If Person A competes or acts assertively, then the reflexive response from Person B will be distrust.

4. If Person A takes aggressive and firm actions, then the reflexive response from Person B will be passive resistance.

5. If Person A is frank, forthright, and takes critical actions, then the reflexive response from Person B will be hostility.

6. If Person A is unconventional and rebellious in a justified way, then the reflexive response from Person B will be punishment.

7. If Person A is skeptical, wary, but realistic, then the reflexive response from Person B will be rejection.

8. If Person A acts shy or sensitive, then the reflexive response from Person B will be arrogance.

9. If Person A does one's duty, obeys, or is modest, then the reflexive response from Person B will be leadership.

10. If Person A respects, admires, or conforms, then the reflexive response from Person B will be advice.

11. If Person A asks for help and trusts, then the reflexive response from Person B will be helping.

12. If Person A agrees, participates, and cooperates, then the reflexive response from Person B will be tenderness.

13. If Person A is affectionate and takes friendly actions, then the reflexive response from Person B will be love.

14. If Person A supports, sympathizes, or treats gently, then the reflexive response from Person B will be acceptance.

15. If Person A helps and gives, then the reflexive response from Person B will be trust.

16. If Person A guides, advises, and teaches, then the reflexive response from Person B will be respect.

Leary arranged the sixteen reflexes in gradations so that Reflex 16 is one gradation from Reflex 1, just as Reflex 7 is one gradation from Reflex 8. Moreover, Leary believed that reflexes are exhibited repeatedly between individuals, the result being a strengthening of the stimulus-response bond.

To consider the validity of Leary's theory, we must consciously monitor our own interpersonal relations given the reminder that many reflexes occur below the level of awareness. Think, for example, of those people from whom you receive arrogant responses. Do you trigger the arrogant reflex by acting "shy," "sensitive," or "modest"? In other words, what Leary is saying is that if you go about this world asking to have your hands slapped, someone will oblige you. In like manner, if you rebel even in a justified way, you can expect punishment.

Existential Theories

It is probably best to introduce Martin Buber's and Carl Rogers' Existential theories by first discussing Soren Kierkegaard (see Popkin and Stroll, 1956), the "father" of existentialism. In the first half of the nineteenth century, the Christian theologian Kierkegaard asked and answered some basic questions.

- What is the point of life?
- What is the purpose of human events?
- What is the meaning of human existence?

Kierkegaard's answers to these questions were:
- There is no point.
- There is no purpose.
- There is no meaning.

Life is absurd, meaningless, and anguished according to Kierkegaard. Nothing is certain. Traditional forms of knowledge cannot be trusted, particularly empirical knowledge, that is, knowledge acquired through sense experience or observation. Even the knowledge acquired through thought and reasoning, rational knowledge, is suspect. The only form of knowledge of which we can be absolutely sure is that which comes from enlightenment. This form of knowledge is miraculous; it comes from God. At the moment of enlightenment, what one knows is absolutely certain, it is eternal. A moment of enlightenment is a change from ignorance to knowledge and the moment is decisive.

Will we be enlightened? There are no assurances that we will be. The best we can do is to be open and desire enlightment.

Often when we have been enlightened we must take what is called the "existential leap" into absurdity. Here we accept a belief blindly and irrationally, possibly in the face of overwhelming contradictory evidence. Kierkegaard is responsible for the statement, "I believe that which is absurd." In fact, the test of one's belief is whether or not it can be held in the face of overwhelming evidence to the contrary.

The philosophy of Kierkegaard lay essentially dormant until the end of the Second World War. It then rose again from the ashes of war-torn Europe. Indeed, the death, destruction, and misery of post-war Europe all seemed to echo the words of Kierkegaard: "There is no point to life," "There is no meaning," and "There is no purpose." All is despair. Writers like Sartre, for example, promulgated this despair.

For those for whom this is the first exposure to the existential view, the feeling of gloom and doom may arise. This is not altogether surprising since existentialism has been called the philosophy of despair. In the following material, the existential philosophy will be related to communication.

Buber's Existential Theory

Less despairing, however, was the existential Jewish theologian, Martin Buber. Buber (1970) categorized human communication in three ways: I-It, I-You, and I-Thou communication.

I-It communication is very similar to human communication with a machine or object. It is a monologue. The two participants are not taking each other into account, but are offering directives to one another. A parking lot attendant shouts his orders to entering drivers, for instance. There is essentially no interaction, but, instead, just directives.

I-You communication is that communication observed in business and social encounters, and in many friendships. There is a sense of dialogue; each participant is taking the others into account. Dinner with friends, meeting with an insurance agent, talking with an instructor, and working with a colleague might be examples of I-You encounters.

I-Thou is the category most responsible for placing Buber's system in the existential camp. An I-Thou relationship is almost mysterious. It is characterized by spontaneity and great mutual joy and satisfaction. Time stands still and life seems to be worthwhile and to have meaning. The I-Thou relationship is the interpersonal *moment of truth*. It has also been characterized as a *peak experience*.

How can an I-Thou relationship be achieved? It cannot be achieved by training. Neither can it be willed into existence. We cannot say, for example, "I will have an I-Thou relationship." I-Thou relationships just happen. The most we can do is to be open to their occurrence, just as Kierkegaard said that we must be open to enlightenment. Sometimes they occur with a stranger and sometimes they may occur with a non-human. Buber's first I-Thou experience occurred while he was petting his horse.

Even enemies may at some point in their involvement experience an I-Thou relationship when at the same moment they gaze upon one another and feel a mutual respect and joy.

Just as I-Thou relationships just happen, so do they abruptly end, leaving behind a memory etched with the knowledge that life is worthwhile and does have meaning. I-Thou relationships are not only related to Kierkegaard's enlightment, but also are similar to Berne's stage of true intimacy because of their transient nature and in the way that they characterize ideal interpersonal relationships.

Rogers' Existential Theory

Another theorist who can fit comfortably in the existential camp is Carl Rogers (1951), a well-known psychotherapist and writer. Although sometimes labeled a phenomenologist, meaning that he believes that one's own experience provides the most basic and valid information on which to act, the labeling does not in any way remove him from existentialism. Indeed, phenomenology and existentialism are closely related since both imply that internal experience provides the only basis on which to act. Often, in fact, the two terms are hyphenated, existential-phenomenology, and thus used as a single term.

Rogers believed that the individual is the locus of all experience. The totality of one's experience is called the *phenomenal field,* a field residing within the individual. In infancy the field is one, a unified whole, but as the child develops, the phenomenal field is partitioned into two parts: 1) *self,* and 2) the remaining *phenomenal field.* A key concept for Rogers is *congruence* which refers to the correspondence between the conscious self and the rest of the phenomenal field. When a person's self is consistent with the remainder of the phenomenal field, there is congruence; incongruence occurs when one's self is not in agreement with the rest of the phenomenal field. To be in the role of spouse but internally not wanting to be in that role creates incongruence. The removal of incongruence is effected by removing all threats from the incongruent person's environment.

Threats are eliminated from the environment by taking a position of *unconditional positive regard* toward the incongruent individual. In taking this position, one does not criticize or censure the incongruent individual's statements or behaviors. An environment is created in which defensiveness is unnecessary. By advocating the position of unconditional positive regard, Rogers assumes that at the core of every individual is a positive person seeking to be *actualized.* Briefly, to be actualized is to enhance one's self, to become autonomous, and to grow.

Although Rogers applied his ideas primarily in the therapeutic setting, he also believed that taking a position of unconditional positive regard should be the basis for all human relationships.

Accordingly, the qualities of ideal communication are:

- The communicators are perceived as trustworthy, or consistently dependable.
- They express their separate selves unambiguously.
- They possess positive attitudes of warmth and caring for others.
- A person in a relationship keeps his or her own separate identity, and permits the other to do the same.
- A relationship is marked by empathy.
- In a relationship one accepts the various facets of the other's experience as communicated by the other.
- Persons in relationships respond with sufficient sensitivity to allay threat to others.
- In relationships people should be able to free themselves from the threat of evaluation by others.
- Communicators recognize that others are changing and are flexible enough to permit others to change.

Summary of Existential Approaches

In the existential approaches discussed, the notions of uncertainty and freedom are stressed. Human relations are uncertain in that we can only be open to the occurrence of ideal relationships and cannot create them on command. Freedom is stressed in that we must allow another person to reach a greater congruence independent of any criticism or advocacy.

At the same time, though, the existential view has provided a philosophically-sanctioned shelter for individuals who perhaps need professional help. To say that sociopathic behavior or self-destructive behavior is merely the result of an existential decision may deprive individuals of the help they need. Moreover, it may not be possible to maintain a position of unconditional positive regard toward another if the other person's behavior is threatening and disruptive. Perhaps this should be reserved for the therapeutic setting. In summary, then, existential theory is based on the assumption that we are all trapped in this existence of life from which escape is made possible only by enlightenment or solitary decision making. Interpersonally, the greatest enlightenment or moment of truth occurs in the I-Thou relationship, according to Buber, and when individuals take positions of positive unconditional regard toward one another, according to Rogers.

Rogers is sometimes called the "happy existentialist" since he believed that there is a good person inside everyone, a person who will indeed emerge if only a non-threatening environment can be created.

Laing's Perception Theory

R.D. Laing was a psychiatrist whose major interest was in schizophrenia. He received a great deal of notoriety when he declared that schizophrenia was not an illness but a logical response by an individual to a set of circumstances. To Laing, the most logical thing for a person to do at times is to go crazy. Critics of Laing say that he has certainly practiced what he has preached. Because of his unorthodox views, Laing has been labeled an antipsychiatrist. Laing has also been criticized for his rambling, schizophrenic-type "word-salad" concerts that he gave on college campuses and in public halls. On the way from clinical psychiatrist to public entertainer, Laing wrote *Interpersonal Perception* with Phillipson and Lee (Laing et al., 1972). This was Laing's most comprehensive work and deals with interpersonal communication from the perceptual standpoint.

According to Laing, the central theme of Interpersonal Perception "is the experiences, perceptions, and actions which occur when two human beings are engaged in a meaningful encounter." The ideal relationship between two individuals is one of understanding. Failure at achieving this ideal is caused by faulty communication. Specifically, communication breaks down because of perceptual spirals created between the interactants.

Laing talked about three kinds of interpersonal perceptions or perspectives. First, there is the *direct perspective*. This is an individual's perception of self, of another person, or of some thing. Next, there are *metaperspectives*. Metaperspectives are perceptions of another's perception. Finally, there are metametaperspectives. To take a metametaperspective is to perceive your partner's perception of your own perception. Higher order perspectives can be imagined but seldom occur in everyday life and are not explored by Laing. To review the perspectives, look at the formats below.

- Direct Perspective: I perceive....
- Metaperspective: I perceive that you perceive....
- Metametaperspective: I perceive that you perceive that I perceive....

The recitation of the perspectives may seem quite complicated. However, in human encounters, the perspectives are made with ease. A young school-age child can be heard to say, "I think that you think that I am mad at you." In this statement the child is expressing a metametaperspective, that is, I perceive that you perceive that I have a negative perception of you. An adult might say, "I can see that you like your new apartment." This is a metaperspective. I perceive that you have a positive perception of your new apartment, The statement, "I like your apartment" would, of course, be a direct perspective.

Using the three perspectives, Laing developed three concepts of understanding.

- *Understanding*: the conjunction between the metaperspective of one person and the direct perspective of the other.
- *Being Understood*: the conjunction between the metametaperspective of one person and the metaperspective of the other.
- *Feeling of being understood*: the conjunction of one's own direct perspective with one's own metametaperspective.

- The word, "conjunction," can be equated with "agreement" or "congruence."

Ideal communication occurs, according to Laing, when there is understanding between two individuals and when each of the individuals is being understood. This means that there is agreement or conjunction between various combinations of their respective perspectives.

To have the feeling of being understood is an index of self-concept. A person may have a poor self-concept if one's direct perspective does not agree with one's metametaperspective. On the other hand, the higher the agreement, the more positive the self-concept.

Communication breaks down when understanding does not occur, or is poor, or when the interactants are not being understood. Breakdowns are thus due to faulty perceptions. The buildup of faulty perceptions is called a *spiral*. For example, if Jack believes that Jill does not love him (metaperspective), but Jill does love him (direct perspective), there is a lack of understanding. Given this one spiral, other spirals can develop. To repair communication breakdowns, spirals must be broken. Clinically this is done in therapy. Outside the clinical situation, spirals are broken by members of a pair attempting to bring as many perceptions as possible to the direct level and then sharing these direct perspectives.

For the small group communicator Laing's message is that we never have direct access to another's perceptions. We only have metaperspectives and metametaperspectives, i.e., we can only perceive another's perceptions; we do not have direct access to them. This introduces possibility for error. We have perceptions of others but indeed these perceptions may be wrong and as a result a spiral of misunderstanding might emerge.

Goffman's Dramaturgical Theory

For Goffman (1963, 1961, 1959) the reason for communicating is clear: *The social imperative to impress other people in one way or another is the single most abiding and pervasive human need.* And Goffman offers no apologies for this strong statement. According to Goffman, communication is all about impression formation. No punches are pulled. All communication is strategic, manipulative, and designed to impress. For example:

- Hosts will deny the fact that they were up most of the night preparing for a dinner party, saying instead, "It was nothing." Why? Because truly competent people do everything with ease.
- Likewise, hosts save the best silver and china for guests.
- People on the job will often try to look busy when they are not. A brisk walk down the corridor is made just to give that impression.
- A couple pays more for a car or house than they can afford to make an impression.
- Someone buys a scarf at an expensive shop just to be able to sew the prestigious label on another garment.
- A student displays great interest in cell biology to impress a professor.
- A veteran reconstructs his war record while a non-veteran creates one.
- Job applicants "pad" and "sweeten" their resumes.

Goffman used the theater as the basis for his communication theory and, thus, the theory is called a dramaturgical theory. It draws from Shakespeare.

All the world's a stage. And all the men and women merely players. They have their exits and their entrances. And people in their time play many parts.

We are all actors; we all play roles; and our goal is to impress the *audience,* an audience which can be one person or many. *Roles* are the activities we engage in when fulfilling the demands of a position created by society. Common roles are mother, father, son, daughter, worker, sexual partner, citizen, guest, host, mourner, and student, to name just a few. Like the actor on stage we all perform and are judged by the audience on how well we perform our role. Like the actor on stage, we must impress the audience. This, of course, is done through communication.

Audiences are always looking for flaws in the performance. Flaws can be verbal or nonverbal. The politician trying to identify with a town mispronounces the name of the town, the cleric forgets a common prayer, the groom has a pimple on his face on his wedding day, the server spills the wine. All are examples of a flawed performance. Sometimes players must communicate with a "stiff upper lip" and reluctantly play the expected role. Retirees who really do not want to retire must play the expected roles at the retirement party and tell how they look forward to the next stage in life, a next stage that, of course, includes death. Similarly, parents of a bride who thought their daughter could have done much better must play the role of proud new in-laws even uttering the stock phrase, "We didn't lose a daughter, we gained a son." All these actions are performed to gain audience approval.

Goffman has said that a *self* awaits the individual entering a role, and that the individual need only conform to the role and its associated pressures and demands to find a "me" ready made. Without a role we do not have a self. You may recall in Chapter 1 we presented the Goffman paradox: Doing is being; if you don't do, you're nothing. Highlighted again is the importance of doing and filling a role. In our society after someone asks your name, invariably the next question is, "What do you do?" If you do not have an answer to that question you may experience a diminished sense of self. And, of course, you not only need to fill roles, but you must also play those roles well.

In groups, specifically task groups, the roles members play are primarily task roles and social-emotional roles. To play a task role well, group members must impress others with the research they have done, maybe carrying the latest journals or a pile of computer print-outs as props; they will want to look serious and introduce good ideas at the right time, and they might in very subtle ways denigrate the ideas of others by suggesting a few modifications that will eventually either destroy the ideas as good tries, or maybe turn the ideas into their own. And, of course, they show that they are not "all work and no play" people by making humorous remarks and smiling at times, and occasionally they show looks of care and concern giving comfort and support to others. And as they do all these things, they will be sincere, honest, and forthright. Why? It impresses the audience.

Goffman said that people wear many masks and whip them on and off as the situation demands. Can you take off all those masks and find the real you? "No," says Goffman. Rip off one mask and there is another mask. This is similar to the statement often made about Hollywood. "What do you find in Hollywood after you strip away all the tinsel and papier-mache? More tinsel and papier-mache."

McGinty's Group Rank Theory

Sarah McGinty (see Martin, 1998) is concerned with how our communication in a group indicates that we do or do not have power.

Group members who possess power will:

- Speak at length.
- Set the agenda for the conversation.
- Stave off interruptions.
- Argue openly.
- Make jokes and laugh.
- Offer solutions, programs, or plans.

Group members who lack power will:

- Drop into conversations.
- Encourage other speakers.
- Ask numerous questions.
- Avoid arguments.
- Rely on gestures, nodding, and smiling to suggest agreement.

It can be seen from the above lists that the powerful are not facilitators, encouragers, and people who share the glory. And, behaviors may be perceived as desirable in some social, self-help, and therapeutic groups, that are perceived as weakness in task groups. McGinty has noted that everyone has come home at one time or another and said, "I offered a great idea but no one heard me and then Penelope offered the same idea later and everyone thought it was hers."

What can you do to avoid being a "Lack Power" Person?

THE DOs

- Analyze meetings. Determine who gets listened to and why, who directs the course of the discussion, who gets noticed and why.
- Analyze your own language habits.
- Analyze ideas, not people.

THE DON'Ts

- Seek collaboration; e.g., "As Wally said…." or "I pretty much agree with Carla."
- Use disclaimers, e.g., "I may be way off base here but…."
- Worry about offending someone.
- Attack people.

You should note from the above that McGinty's views stand in contrast to those of other theorists. She would disagree, for example, with Berne's and Carnegie's recommendations about communication. In short, she would see some of their recommendations as indicating weakness.

Theoretical Reflections

As you read the descriptions of the above theories you may have come to the conclusion that the theorists, in the main, see human communication in general and small group communication in particular as a cynical and manipulative process. Berne talked about games in which one communicator sees another as a mark or victim thereby making every message a move in the game, a step in reaching a goal. And even though the player's messages may be kind, considerate, and nurturing, it is merely part of the set-up.

Gordon talked about the strategy of restructuring our speech to communicate more effectively. Carnegie would have us shower other people with flattery and praise in an effort to bring them around to our way of thinking. The existentialists believe that whether or not one experiences ideal communication is a chance situation; one can be open to the possibility but there are no guarantees. For Goffman, making impressions is everything and McGinty sees the task group as a Darwinian swamp where the strong dominate the weak.

Is there any sincerity and honesty anywhere in the communication arena, and would you want to be in a group with the totally sincere and honest person? Imagine how totally sincere and honest people would communicate in a group. They would tell you they don't like your hair, your clothing, the way you talk, your ideas, for instance. You probably would tire of this mode of communication very quickly. On the other hand you do not want people to communicate with you when they have hidden agendas, where every exchange is just a move in a game to get something from you: your influence, access to your network, your free labor, your submission to satisfy sexual or power needs, or your money.

Most people settle for something between the extreme communication styles outlined above. We like to hear people say, "Hello! Good to see you," even though we know there may be a bit of insincerity in the statement. We like compliments, we like cheerful people, we like people who listen to us. We know that the compliments are not always sincere, that the complimenter is not always cheerful, and the person who appears to be listening to us may indeed not be. These rather benign but nonetheless somewhat phony messages are often referred to as *social lubricants;* they "grease" social interaction and make it run more smoothly. It may be a group member's obligation to bring some grease to the table.

The point of all this is that in a group or team not all communication is totally sincere, honest, or authentic. People would probably not tolerate this kind of communication for long. It would be seen as impolite and unkind.

As we talk in a group we are concerned with being liked, being perceived as bright and competent and as decision makers and leaders, for instance. All of our concerns are only realized through communication. Therefore, we plan our messages to bring about those realizations. We become strategic communicators.

Summary

In this chapter the concept of *theory* was introduced and a number of communication theories were presented and discussed. The theories were those of Berne, Gordon, Carnegie, Leary, Buber, Rogers, Laing, Goffman, and McGinty. The diversity of views across the theories supports the notion that theorists can agree upon the communication behaviors observed in a group or team, but they can have, at the same time, markedly different interpretations of those behaviors.

CHAPTER 4

VERBAL COMMUNICATION IN GROUPS AND TEAMS

In the last chapter we looked at a number of theories of human communication, the implications of those theories, and what theories suggest for group communicators who want to improve their skills. In this chapter and the next we will become more analytic and discuss the codes of communication: in this chapter the verbal or language code, and, in the next, the nonverbal code. As is the convention, we will equate verbal and language communication so that any time verbal is mentioned, language could be substituted for verbal and vice versa.

We define *language* as a system of symbols known by at least two individuals. Language can be expressed through speech, writing, and signing as in American Sign Language (ASL), e.g. Thus language can be received through listening, reading, and visual reading of ASL. All natural languages (English, Spanish, Vietnamese, etc.) have a systematic *structure*. They are structured in the ways they build larger linguistic units from smaller units. For example, in English word order is important: "Dog bites man," is different from "Man bites dog." In other languages word order is less important. In Latin, for instance, certain words are inflected, that is, given different endings to show their function in the sentence thus reducing the importance of word order.

A language is *symbolic*. A *symbol* is a sign that stands in an arbitrary relationship with its referent, that is, the thing referred to. *Arbitrary* means that there is no fixed relationship between the sign and the referent. For example, the symbol, "chair," was in no way determined by the physical thing we sit on. In fact, we could call it anything we like as long as people agree on it. And, of course, people who speak different languages have different names for the same thing. Germans, for example, call the thing we sit on "der Stuhl."

The fact that there is this arbitrary relationship between the word and the referent opens the door to a number of language phenomena. These phenomena and their implications for group and team communication will be discussed.

Language As A Model of The Universe

With a Ph.D. in chemical engineering in hand, Benjamin Lee Whorf (See Carroll, 1964) became a fire inspector for a large insurance company. In his travels he noted that workers would not smoke around drums marked "full" but would smoke around drums marked "empty." Of course this was a tragic mistake for the "empty" drums were far more dangerous since gasoline fumes are far more explosive than the liquid gasoline. This observation of the "empty-full" behavior aroused Whorf's interest in language and led him to study language and culture, collaborating at times with Edward

Sapir. The Whorf-Sapir Theory of Linguistic Relativity emerged from their collaboration. A brief description of this theory follows.

Whorf assumed that there are an infinite number of stimuli in the world but that our brain has only a finite capacity. This means that we are hopelessly overwhelmed; there is simply too much to deal with. One solution is to categorize the stimuli, that is, we call some things chairs, and ignore the differences among individual chairs. In this way we do not overload our brain by trying to find a new name for every chair in the world (for in fact no two chairs are exactly alike).

Therefore, *categorization* of stimuli simplifies our life and we categorize by using language.

Whorf found that people use language to categorize or simplify the world. Different groups categorize in different ways based upon what is important for the group. For example, for Trobriand Islanders yams are the staff of life and, as a result, an elaborate yam vocabulary developed; for Eskimos and some skiers snow is very important and led to the creation of an elaborate snow vocabulary. For the Westerner a yam is just something bought at the market and the person simply cannot "see" or "know" about the yam as does the Trobriand Islander. They live in two different worlds. Whorf was fond of saying that your language is your map of the territory. What he meant by that is that there is a physical world that is potentially open for everyone to know, but there is too much to know so through language we categorize and pay most attention to the things important to us and ignore things less important. Our language, in short, is our map of the territory. But Whorf reminds us that just as there can be many maps for any territory, street maps, road maps, topographical maps, demographic maps, subterranean maps, there are many language maps, English, French, German, Japanese, Russian and Spanish, for instance. No map covers all the territory and by not doing so it gives its user only one view of the world. Whorf believed that the language you speak determines the way you think and perceive so all your thoughts and perceptions are relative to your language. Other language users think and perceive in different ways.

These different ways of thinking and perceiving or seeing the world are most contrasted between different languages. Whorf contrasted the languages of native North Americans, the Hopi, for example, with the languages of their European conquerors, noting how members of the two groups could be in the same physical environment but truly living in two different worlds. At the same time, within the same language culture we can see some Whorfian effects. For example, members of any specialty, be it medicine or mechanics, learn elaborate vocabularies to direct their perception and thought so that they literally live in a world different from the world of lay people; the specialists and lay people can be looking at the same human body or the same automobile but the specialists see things to which lay people are "blind."

What is Whorf's message for small group and team communication?

1. Group members have only partial views of the world and these views are determined by the languages they speak

2. Members must assume there are other views of the world, views to which they are "blind."

3. Group members should try to have these other, unknown views of the world, made known to them through invited guests, research, travel, and so on. By getting as many views of the world or maps of the territory as possible, a group can improve its creativity and problem-solving skills.

General Semantics

Semantics refers to the study of meaning and *General Semantics* is a branch of semantics which focuses on the effects of words and labels on people's perceptions, attitudes, feelings, and behaviors. Words and labels can affect the way we perceive ourselves and others; they can affect our attitudes or our predispositions to believe and act; they can determine how we feel, triggering any one of a range of emotions; and they can affect our behavior, mobilizing us to go in one direction or another. Many people have contributed to the General Semantics literature; we can only sample from this vast literature to support the general semanticists' position.

Self-Fulfilling Prophecy

Rosenthal (see Tauber, 1997) completed studies in which elementary school children were given an IQ test with an impressive name, "The Harvard Test of Inflected Acquisition." The actual scores of these tests, however, were not given to the teachers. Instead, the teachers were told that certain students were expected to bloom and were labeled "bloomers." The teachers accepted these labels and believed them, just assuming that the children so labeled were quite capable of learning. The teachers taught them accordingly. The children did indeed learn, in fact, beyond the expectations that their actual test scores suggested.

The net effect of labeling the children as "bloomers" affected the teachers' perceptions and attitudes toward the children and mobilized the teachers to behave in a manner that assumed the children could and would learn. This effect is known as the *self-fulfilling prophecy*, and Tauber says, "What the self-fulfilling prophecy process does is label someone and then have that person treated as if that label were correct." And earlier, according to Tauber, Merton described the concept as follows: "The self-fulfilling prophecy is, in the beginning, a false definition of the situation evoking a new behavior which makes the originally false conception come true." The whole process begins with words and thereby testifies to the power of words.

Stuttering

There is a general semantic theory about the cause of stuttering. Johnson (1946), the creator of this theory, believed that stuttering begins in the parent's ear and not in the child's mouth. By this Johnson meant that parents interpret normal dysfluencies in their child's speech as stuttering and label the child as a stutterer, begin to treat the child as a stutterer, and as a result the child begins to stutter. The parents may never use the word, "stutterer", but nonetheless, the label or concept is in their minds and affects their behavior. When the child's speech exhibits dysfluencies that are normal for a child learning to speak, the parents are thinking "stuttering" and consequently exhibit a variety of anxiety responses which are transferred to the child who becomes anxious as a result and indeed may begin to stutter. It is important to repeat that the whole process can occur without the words, "stutterer" or "stuttering," ever being spoken.

The Placebo Effect

When a new drug is being tested, the clinical trials include giving some patients the real drug and others a *placebo* or sugar pill encapsulated to look like the real drug. The drug and the placebo are administered in a *double blind* manner, meaning that neither the dispenser of the drug nor the patient knows which is the real drug and which is the placebo. Pill dispensers are not told and are kept "blind" to whether they are dispensing the real drug or the placebo in order that they do not verbally or nonverbally transmit the message that this will or will not help. Similarly, patients are kept "blind" to what they are taking so that they maintain the belief that what they are taking will have therapeutic value. Why is this done? The simple answer is that if one is given a pill (even a placebo) and led to believe that it has therapeutic value, it often does have therapeutic effects. Somehow some healing process is triggered by the label, "pill," and the physical reality of the pill. Frank (1974) listed a number of pathologies that respond positively to placebos alone. Included in Frank's list are both physical and psychopathologies.

Anecdotes

Other General Semantic effects can be found in the following anecdotes.

- A four-and-a-half-year-old girl goes to the dentist. At the end of the session the dentist says, "You did so well today I thought you were at least five years old." The little girl is on Cloud Nine, talking about it on the way home and rushing to tell her father. The five-year-old label elevated her self-esteem.

- Clerks in retail stores are no longer clerks but associates, a label that is supposed to make them part of the team with decision-making power.

- Weapons of mass destruction are called "Peacemakers" in the hope of changing attitudes about the weapon.

- Virtually all weapons are called defensive weapons suggesting that no war will ever be initiated. How could it? There are no offensive weapons.

- And the label, "War Department," has been changed to "Department of Defense."

- Tax increases are called "revenue enhancements" in the hope that voters will react less angrily to the higher taxes.

- Patients are often labeled according to their prognoses, "terminal," for example, or according to diagnosis, "There's a kidney in 404."

- Hospital floors are often referred to by patient prognosis; "That's terminal up on ten."

These labels affect the way staff members perceive and treat patients, often in negative and dehumanizing ways.

Implications

What can the small group and team communicator learn from the general semanticist?

1. Words and labels are powerful tools; they can have tremendous effects, effects that may be both positive and negative.

2. These effects can be used to enhance the self-concept of others and to motivate them to perform beyond their expectations or they can be used to lower self-concept and inhibit good performances. These are personal effects.

3. Words and labels can help a group or team see a problem differently, to see it as less daunting, and, thus, more amenable to a solution. Alcoholism was relabeled as a medical problem from a behavioral one by many treatment specialists. As a result of re-labeling, the problem is now viewed from within a medical model with corresponding diagnosis and treatment regimens. Perceptions of the problem as behavioral or criminal are erased.

Metaphor

A *metaphor* is a very powerful figure of speech. When we use a metaphor, we say something is analogous to something else, and we make this comparison in the hope that what we know about the latter can be applied to the former in order to help us understand the former. In his book, *The Body in Question*, Miller (1978) noted that metaphors were very powerful tools in understanding the human body. We didn't know much about the heart until the water pump was invented, and little about the brain until switchboards and computers were developed. Aiding medical researchers, therefore, were the metaphors: the heart is a pump, the nerves are electrical lines, and the brain is a computer. The philosopher, Francis Bacon, had a preference for insect metaphors. He compared philosophers in the Aristotelian tradition to spiders, always weaving a web, enticing, and ensnaring their prey in little word games that never lead to practical knowledge. On the other hand, he compared the experimental method practitioners to bees, animals that go out and gather the pollen (data), process it (data analysis), and then turn it into honey (results that have practical use). In recent years, the spider's web metaphor, of course, has been most prominent with the internet. Developed as a failsafe system that could remain operational even if part of it suffered damage, the internet has all the characteristics of a web with a worldwide span of threads and nodes.

In small groups and teams the use of metaphors can facilitate group productivity. For example, a group working on a problem might say, "Let's pretend that this is a timed test; we have two hours to do the test so we have to do something." Here the test is the metaphor. It is a metaphor for the group's task. We take the characteristics of a test and apply them to the problem-solving situation. A second example relates to a group that was considering recommended policies related to prenuptial agreements. One half of the group was assigned to look at the negative aspects of prenuptial agreements. This group chose the jail as their metaphor, applying all the negative aspects of being in jail to signing a prenuptial agreement. The other half of the group looked at the positive side of prenuptial agreements and used a road map as its metaphor. The map details how to go from Point A to Point B and the prenuptial agreement, in kind, details how a married couple is going to live its life from marriage to death or divorce. Therefore, metaphors can be very helpful in thinking about problems. They can help to give structure and focus to the problem, and they can help to raise crucial points about a problem that would otherwise be hidden from the group had a metaphor not been introduced, wittingly or unwittingly. In a later chapter, in fact, we will see that a commonly accepted idea generation technique is called the metaphorical thinking technique.

Other functions of metaphors that can improve group performance are:

1. Metaphors make discussion more vivid and colorful. A person who is a bit unstable, for example, can be described as unstable, or can be described more vividly, as a "loose cannon," a "quart low," a "less than full deck," a gas stove whose "pilot light has gone out," and so on. While the metaphor may not always be fair, it can liven up the discussion nonetheless.

2. Metaphors can facilitate the remembering process. This may be due to the fact that metaphors create pictures in the mind and visual images can contribute to the remembering of associated linguistic information. Also involved is the emotional factor. Metaphors often trigger an emotional reaction, either positive or negative, and emotion and memory are yoked together. Think of any traumatic event that you experienced and you will probably remember the most minute details of anything you saw, heard, or did on that day.

3. Metaphors can motivate. A group may describe itself as the Ferrari of groups and characterize an opposing or competitive group as the Yugo. Here the Ferrari metaphor can help the group members think of speed, agility, and sleekness and then behave accordingly. They can see their Yugo competitors as small, slow, unreliable, unattractive, and so on.

4. Metaphors can help a group when it communicates for an external audience. The metaphor can facilitate understanding. For example, a most commonly used metaphor in group presentations is the pie chart. A presenting group may say that the total expenditures for a given period of time were a certain amount. This represents the whole pie. Then the pie is cut into pieces of various sizes, each piece representing a given expenditure. The pie metaphor is a very effective communication tool.

Other Figures of Speech

A metaphor is a figure of speech; it is one of a number of figures of speech, some of which are very similar to the metaphor. Figures of speech beyond the metaphor are:

1. *Personification:* Personification attributes life and action to inanimate objects: *The sky is smiling today.*

2. *Simile:* A simile expresses the resemblance which one object bears to another: *He runs like a deer.*

3. *Allegory:* An allegory is the relation of fictitious events to convey or illustrate important truths: Examples are: *Animal Farm* and *Aesop's Fables.*

4. *Vision:* A vision represents past or future events as taking place at the present*: I see the dagger before me.*

5. *Hyperbole:* Hyperbole represents things as greater or less, better or worse than they actually are: *Faster than a speeding bullet. Touching the heavens.*

6. *Irony:* Irony is language that means the contrary of what the words import: *John? (pause) Is a student?*

7. *Metonymy:* Metonymy puts the cause for the effect or the effect for the cause: *Gray hairs should be respected.*

8. *Synecdoche:* Synecdoche is putting a part for the whole or a whole for a part: *He commanded ten sail. The roof protects you.*

9. *Antithesis:* Antithesis is contrasting expressions having different meanings: *Excess of ceremony shows want of breeding.*

10. *Climax:* Climax is the arrangement of the parts of a sentence by which they are made to rise step by step in importance: *It is an outrage to bind a citizen; to scourge him is an atrocious crime; to put him to death is almost a parracide; but to crucify him—what shall I call it?*

11. *Exclamation:* Exclamation is used to express some strong emotion of the mind: *Oh, sacred privilege of citizenship! Once served, but now trampled upon!*

12. *Interrogation:* Interrogation is putting a strong affirmation in the form of a question: *Hath the Lord said it? And shall he not do it? Hath he spoken it? And shall he not make it good?*

13. *Paralepsis:* Paralepsis is calling attention to a thing by pretending to conceal it: *His indolence, to say nothing of his dishonesty, disqualifies him for high pursuits.*

14. *Apostrophe:* Apostrophe is an abrupt turning from the subject to address some object real or imaginary: *Can we not arrest and punish this man? O wretch! O villain! His crimes will yet overtake thee.*

Like metaphor the above figures of speech can serve to make discussions more vivid and colorful, to facilitate the remembering process, to motivate, to communicate to external audiences, and at times can facilitate the problem-solving process.

Connotation and Denotation

While people indeed have commonly shared meanings of words, called *denotative* meanings, they also have meanings that are peculiar to them. These are *connotative* meanings. Often connotative meanings are created as a result of traumatic and emotional experiences. Someone who witnesses a convict die in the electric chair may always have a reaction to "chair" that others do not have, the victim of a serious accident may have a peculiar response to "car," and a person whose house has burned down may have a peculiar reaction to the mention of "house." The author has had two experiences with "house." In one case, a patient in a rehabilitation center responded emphatically, "No!" and began to cry when asked to imitate the sentence, "Sell the house," during a speech and language evaluation. Later, it was learned that her family wanted to sell her house. In the second situation, a woman began to cry at the mention of "house." Here it was later learned that her family home had burned and a family member had perished. While group discussion requires the use of a common vocabulary, group and team members must nonetheless be sensitive to the possibility that even common words may have different connotative meanings for members.

Vagueness

Words can be *vague*, that is the meaning of the word lies somewhere on a continuum. If you were asked, for example, to name a large town and a small town; state the height of a tall and a short man and woman; and tell what number comes to mind when you hear "several" and "many," would your responses be the same as others answering the same question? Probably not. There would be a distribution of differences. In group discussions there is always the potential for misunderstanding due to the vagueness of the words that are used.

Ambiguity

Ambiguous means that a word has at least two meanings. Let us take the word "productive," for example. For some people in a discussion group "productive" means the generation of a large number of ideas, the more ideas generated the more "productive" the group is. For others, "productive" has quite a different meaning. For these individuals quantity is not important but quality is; generating one excellent idea is seen as productive. In fact it is seen as being more productive than the generation of 100 mediocre ideas.

The Pygmalion Effect

The way you speak can have a dramatic effect on how you are perceived. This is called the "Pygmalion Effect," taken from a play of the same name by George Bernard Shaw. The play was later made into a musical and a film, "My Fair Lady." In the play a Cockney girl, Liza Doolittle, sells flowers on the street; she has a terrible accent, according to Professor Higgins who makes a bet with his friend that if he just trained the young woman to speak properly she could pass for royalty. The lessons take place and Liza passes.

Indeed people are judged on the way they speak. Judgments are made about intelligence, knowledge, and so on. Talented people without good speaking skills are often relegated to a group's "back stage" activities and are often passed over for "front stage" duties, particularly when the group represents itself in public.

Revelation Through Language

When people in a group speak, they can unwittingly reveal certain things about themselves. For example, the order in which people mention things often reveals their preference; people frequently name the most important person, place, or thing first and the progressively less important in sequence. In like manner, when people repeatedly bring up certain topics or themes it can often reveal their concerns about the content of the respective topics and themes. You can learn what people worry about, what angers them, and so on. A person who believed that speech can reveal that which has been suppressed and repressed was Sigmund Freud, who catalogued and discussed slips of the tongue in his book, *Psychopathology of Everyday Life.* As previously mentioned, Freud described one of his own slips of the tongue when he was counseling a female patient and ended the session with "Goodbye, Sir." Freud than realized that he was really talking to the woman's husband who, Freud suspected, was eavesdropping at the door.

SUMMARY

There is the phrase that "Sticks and stones may break my bones but words will never hurt me." But words do hurt; they hurt in many ways. And, they can help in many ways. In this chapter we tried to show the dramatic effects words can have. They affect how we see the world, how we perceive, and how we think. They affect how we perform, how we perceive ourselves, and how others perceive us. They can unwittingly reveal. There is an aphorism which states that "A choice of words is a choice of worlds."

We can apply this aphorism to the group and team situation. The right choice of words can help in framing a problem, can help delineate paths to a solution, and can help in communicating the solution to the audience for whom the problem was solved. And, in like manner, the right choice of words can be very instrumental in establishing and maintaining a positive interpersonal climate in the group.

CHAPTER 5

NONVERBAL COMMUNICATION
IN
GROUPS AND TEAMS

Imagine that you are invisible and that you are observing a group discussion. You cannot be seen, heard, or touched. The group discussants are speaking a language you do not know. You cannot, therefore, understand what the people are saying, and thus you are shut out of the social interaction that is taking place. But are you? "Certainly not," would be the answer given by those who study nonverbal behavior. You are missing the speech messages that are generated in our imaginary room, but there are many other types of messages that you can identify and about which you can make inferences. These non-speech messages are called nonverbal messages.

By *nonverbal communication* is meant that form of communication wherein messages are sent by virtue of an agent's physical appearance, adornment, body movements and postures, touching behavior, eye behavior, vocal behavior, utilization of time, design and selection of spatial environments, and choice of objects to fill space.

People who study and write about nonverbal communication often say that *nonverbally you cannot not communicate* or that *nonverbally nothing never happens.* What these somewhat tortuous double-negative phrases tell us is that we are always communicating in the nonverbal medium. Verbally one can stop communicating by simply not talking, for example, but nonverbally we are always "on," communicating the right thing or the wrong thing. We can't communicate nothing.

The nonverbal topic area can be subcategorized into ten subtopic areas: organismics, cosmetics, costuming, kinesics, haptics, oculesics, vocalics, chronemics, proxemics, and objectics.

Organismics

As you watch people interacting in groups and teams you may notice the variety of their physical characteristics. There can be sex, race, and age differences as well as many degrees of height, weight, and personal attractiveness. Messages generated by physical characteristics are called *organismic* messages. Convincing testimony about the impact of organismic messages can be found in the massive human rights efforts on behalf of women, racial minorities, the physically handicapped, and the aged.

Studies of physical height have shown that there is a positive correlation between standing height and intelligence (see Egolf and Corder, 1991). Across studies the correlations hover around a positive .20 and they hold for both males and females. This is not a strong correlation; it means that four percent of one's intelligence can be attributed to one's height. The striking fact is not so much in the strength of this correlation, but in its consistent appearance across many studies. Explanations for the height-IQ link range from those that are *nature based,* (genetically determined) to those that are *nurture based* (determined by life experience).

Whatever lies behind the correlations, taller people are seen as being more competent and are rewarded accordingly. Deck (1968), for example, found that height was a predictor of starting salary for males, those six feet two inches in height and taller receiving starting salaries 12% higher than their under-six-foot peers. More recently, in studies in two large corporations, one profit, the other non-profit, Egolf and Corder (1991) found that managerial women and managerial men were significantly taller than non-managerial women and men respectively.

One aspect of height that cannot be ignored of course is the physical aspect. If someone is taller than you, you must look up to that person and that person will look down at you. This puts you in a subordinate position and the other in a superior position when both you and the other are standing. Fortunately, most group and team deliberations occur in seated positions, which tend to erase height differences, since most of the height dimension is in the legs.

In 1985 scientists introduced synthetic human growth hormone and there was concern that it would be over prescribed. Apparently it was. A *Science News* article (see Growth . . . , 1996) reported that just four out of ten children who got the hormone are actually growth-hormone deficient. This report like many, many others testifies to the importance we place on standing height.

People who are perceived as short are forgiven; it's not their fault. People who are overweight, however, are generally not forgiven. They are often seen as not being in control, lacking willpower and discipline, and not caring about their health. They are sometimes ridiculed, as in the case of a billboard for a health club in San Francisco, which read, "When the aliens come they will eat the fat ones first." This discriminatory billboard led to a public outcry and subsequent municipal legislation to prevent such advertisements in the future.

Asher (2000) reported that in the job interview the overweight person is out of the running and that prejudice against overweight women is most severe. Asher further reported that weight discrimination is much more prevalent in the hiring process than bias against race or gender.

One area of organismics that has been studied extensively is that of physical attractiveness. Thousands of scholarly articles, books, personal accounts, and special television reports have been written on the subject. This storehouse of information supports the notion that physical attractiveness is important across the span of life from birth until death. Attractive young children are seen by their teachers as being more intelligent than their less attractive peers. And the children see attractive teachers as being "smarter" and "nicer" than less attractive teachers, suggesting that the tendency to ascribe more positive characteristics to attractive people begins very early. In fact, Langlois (1991) found that babies as young as three months looked significantly longer at an attractive face when that face was paired with an unattractive face, a finding that led Langlois to conclude that this behavior is "wired in" since the babies were too young to have learned about attractiveness. When the perpetrator of a misdeed is unknown, attractive children are less often blamed than are their less attractive peers. And when the perpetrator of the misdeed is known, the interpretation of the act is more forgiving for the attractive child than for the less attractive.

Attractive adults too are seen as being more intelligent, competent, social, innocent in courtroom situations, and as having better personalities than their less attractive peers. Starting salaries of both attractive men and women are greater than those of their less attractive peers and the differences widen as time goes by.

In the book, *The Body in Question,* Jonathan Miller (1978, p. 16) noted that our bodies are more than premises in which we live; they are in large part who we are. Miller is reminding us of the relationship between our physical manifestation and our sense of self. Who we are is very much determined by our physical selves. Our sheer physical presentation communicates so many organismic messages to observers who react to these messages in turn. These reactions are instrumental in determining our self concept according to Miller. Think of how different your life might have been if your physical features and your appearance would have been different. The physical difference could be slight. For example, it has been said that if Cleopatra's nose had been ¼ of an inch longer or shorter the whole history of the Roman Empire would have been different. The Roman legions did not lose on the Egyptian battlefields but in Cleopatra's bedroom where supposedly her beauty seduced Julius Caesar and Marc Antony and saved Egypt. And, of course, you have probably heard the phrase, "Was this the face that launched a thousand ships?" referring to the beautiful Helen of Troy, a Greek, who, in Greek mythology, was given to the Trojan, Paris, a gift that precipitated the ten-year Trojan War. The Greeks launched their 1000 ships to rescue Helen from Troy.

As you think about group interaction, think about the effects that group members' physical characteristics have on others and on themselves. Physical appearance can indeed affect others as well as contribute to the determination of self.

Cosmetics

Further evidence that physical appearance is important can be found in the ways in which individuals seek to modify themselves through the use of applied cosmetics and cosmetic surgery. This area of nonverbal communication is called *cosmetics*. It is not surprising that people spend so much money on applicative cosmetics (perfumes, colognes, after shaves and potions and lotions in general), and on cosmetic surgery; they want to make themselves attractive in some way since there are so many advantages to being attractive. At one time expenditures on cosmetics and cosmetic surgery were made overwhelmingly by women. But each year more and more men are making those expenditures. And while we may hear of some of the rather dramatic cosmetic surgical procedures undergone by certain celebrities most people who have the procedures done simply want to appear a bit younger, fit, energetic, and well rested. In short, they want a bit of an edge.

Costuming

The branch of nonverbal communication dealing with dress is called *costuming*. Reasons for wearing clothing are seemingly obvious; it is worn for protection, modesty, and utility. Clothing also serves a signaling or communicative function. Uniforms are most distinctive in this regard. Police, priests, nurses, nuns, soldiers, and sailors all communicate their formal, professional roles in life via uniforms. Wearers of non-uniforms communicate a variety of important messages as well. Their clothing tells about their individuality, their group affiliations, their status, and the degree to which they support the social situation or are alienated from it, for example. Male occupational status for years has been communicated through shirt color, blue collar versus white collar. And men's suit coats are impractical garments in which to do physical labor and, therefore, show that the wearer is not in the laboring class. And, of course, recently many professional and businesswomen have adopted the skirted or pants suit, a sign of their occupational status.

In recent years business and professional dress has become more casual, the so-called Silicon Valley look. Some people thought that casual dress meant, "Wear anything you like." But they were wrong. We all wear uniforms and in any situation there is a dress code even if casual dress is encouraged. This code communicates your group affiliation and your support for the group. If you violate this code you will be seen as markedly superior or inferior to the group members, or as alienated from the group. Lee (1995) reported on the lengths to which organizations go to teach their employees how to dress casually. One company had a fashion show to inform employees what is and is not proper casual dress. In addition, the company prepared a report, two-inches thick, that further educated employees on what is appropriate casual dress. Indeed "casual" does not mean wear anything you like; it is simply another dress code.

Once again imagine that you are observing a group. How are the members dressed? Is there a mixture of "suits" and "non-suits"? If there were only one suit would you infer something about the suit wearer's role, leader, manager, visiting consultant and so on. If suit jackets are hanging from the occupants' chairs, and men's ties are loosened and sleeves rolled up, what are the messages compared to all jackets on and men's ties knotted?

Kinesics

Looking at people in a group you can see a variety of postures and body positions as well as the body movements that occur between postures. Communication through body movement is called *kinesic communication*.

Some group members may move together and take like postures. At a table, those seated on one side perhaps all rest their chins in their left hands. People in groups often move in a kind of synchrony. These synchronous movements are partially directed by speech. Both speakers and listeners seem to perform a dance. The body moves in time with speech. Slow-motion films emphasize the elaborateness of these synchronous dances. In addition people move their bodies in synchrony with the body movements of others. Here again a "dance" can occur.

Two basic postures, for example, that have attracted the interest of investigators who study nonverbal communication are extension and contraction. *Extension* is associated with relaxation. *Contraction* is associated with anxiety and fear. These basic postures are used by film-makers. The strong man in a Western, for example, is shown leaning back (extended) over a saloon bar. In this position, the man exudes an air of strength, because is seems that he is relaxed in the face of danger.

Between extension and contraction researchers have identified a number of postures that signal boredom, attentiveness, submissiveness, energy, piety, affiliation, cooperation, competition, flirtatiousness, trust, deception, attitude, and disapproval, for example. Some illustrations follow:

- Group members who have negative attitudes toward one another or who are competing with one another will often sit and stand face-to-face while group members who like one another will often sit and stand side by side.

- If one group member has a negative attitude toward another the holder of the negative attitude will often stand with *arms akimbo* (hands on hips and elbows out like extended fins).

- Group members who have positive attitudes toward one another tend to have more open body postures than those with negative attitudes.

- When there are status differences in a group those of higher status are more relaxed than those of lower status

Haptics

Communication through touch, *haptics communication*, is probably the most basic form of human interaction. During periods of emotional intensity, grief, love, or hatred, we use the tactile modality by reaching out, embracing, or striking, for example. Tactile communication is thought by many to be important in personality development. Evidence from studies of infant monkeys and infant humans suggests that early touch experiences are a determiner of later intellectual and emotional growth. Touch can also be therapeutic. It is believed that touch in the form of massage fosters the release of *endorphins* in the recipient's body; these substances tend to alleviate pain and reduce anxiety.

While touch is seen to have many positive benefits there are at the same time "no touch" directives being issued in many organizations. Organizations fear that they may be charged with tolerating sexual harassment and abuse in their organizations. Kronholz (1998) tells of "no-touch" directives issued in many schools. Teachers are being told, "Don't touch, don't pat, don't tap, and definitely don't hug."

In general when touch patterns are reciprocal between two individuals, it indicates that an affable and symmetrical interpersonal relationship exists; when the patterns are non-reciprocal, the relationship is asymmetrical and less than affable. The latter kind of relationship often exists when there is a status difference between the individuals.

Touch patterns vary across cultures, a fact that makes life interesting for the sojourner and for the person from a non-touch culture who is dating a person from a touch culture. This becomes most interesting when the dating partners meet each other's families for the first time. Whether minimally-touching cultures are less affectionate and friendly than those that abundantly touch is difficult to determine. What is probably true is that cultural forces are durable and that, although the "crash" touch programs popular in some types of encounter group therapy are fascinating, their effects are probably transient and superficial in a minimally-touching culture.

In task groups touching behaviors are, for the most part, minimal because of the taboo aspect of touch in organizations. After the handshake little touching follows. There may be a functional touch now and then, a tap on the shoulder by an entering secretary who brings in an important message, or some high fives when the group shares a positive emotion.

Oculesics

If you were to observe carefully the people in a group you would notice a cascade of glances and eye movements. These glances and movements have rich communicative value, and transmission of information by this means is called *oculesics*. The eye has always been surrounded with mystery. The word, eye, is associated with a curse (the evil eye), truth ("Look me in the eye and say that") and pleasure (a gleam in the eye). Vision is linked verbally with understanding ("I see").

A group can isolate one of its members by not looking at that member or threaten the member by staring at him. Generally, too, people look at what they like, describable by paraphrasing a biblical passage: Where the eye is, there is the heart also. So who looks at whom can provide important information.

Most commonly people use their eyes to show, through eye contact, that they are paying attention. High-status people usually receive more visual attention than they give. In a group certain factors are somewhat under the control of the group members' eyes. For example, when a speaker relinquishes the floor, the person most likely to speak next is the one at whom the speaker looked last. More fascinating perhaps are the eye "editorials" composed in groups. While one person speaks, others often signal agreement, disagreement, or disgust by subtle eye movements. Little editorials continually form, bubble, and burst.

Other communicative eye movements include the loss of eye contact by a person when the person is asked a question requiring thought, and an increase in blinking when one becomes anxious. Normally when resting we blink about 15 times per minute to bathe the eyes. Blinking rates markedly above 15 can indicate a person is under great stress. Blink counts are often used to gauge the stress debating political candidates are under when asked certain questions.

Finally, with elaborate equipment it is possible to observe dilation and contraction of the pupil of the eye. Researchers have shown that the pupil dilates when the eye apprehends something pleasurable and contracts when the stimulus is innocuous or unpleasant. These findings about pupillary reaction may begin to unravel some of the previously mentioned mysteries surrounding the eye.

Vocalics

Vocalics refers to the effects of the voice on communication. Not included in vocalics are the words a speaker is saying; instead it is the quality, loudness, pitch, time patterning, and stress patterning of the voice that accompanies speech that is the focus of vocalics.

Vocalics is especially important insofar as the affective (emotional) content of a message is concerned. Many times the linguistic message of speech is contradicted vocally. For example, someone who screams, "No, I'm not defensive!" contradicts the linguistic message by the manner of expression. When a contradiction occurs, most listeners give credibility to the vocalic nonverbal message instead of the linguistic one. If someone looks and sounds angry, and says, "I'm very angry," for example, the verbal and nonverbal messages complement each other.

In general the research supports the old aphorism, "It's not what was said but how it was said that mattered." For example, research has shown that whether or not a patient complies with a physician's recommendation may depend upon the physician's voice. And in like manner it has been shown that the way a research subject participates in an experiment may be dependent upon how the subject is greeted vocally when entering the experimental situation. In a group, voices of the members can indicate the members' emotional states. The voice can indicate the degree to which a member is supportive or non-supportive of a proposal. Voices can signal the imminence or existence of interpersonal conflict in the group. In short, the vocalic patterns of group members provide a good barometer of the emotional climate of the group.

Chronemics

When visiting a physician or a superior we often wait past the appointed hour, sometimes long past. The physician or superior, however, does not wait for us. Something is communicated by time. In this case, it is status. Indeed, the nature of a relationship often can be defined by who waits for whom and for how long. Transmission of information through use of time is called *chronemics*.

In a group people talk for varying lengths of time. Some people hold the floor longer than others do. The inference, of course, is that they are more important than the others. People spar over time by interrupting one another. By breaking into a statement the interrupter blatantly tells the interrupted person that his or her message is of low value, that "I am dominant, you are submissive."

Time management is crucial in group meetings. Proper management can result in members being satisfied with a meeting, and feeling that the group was successful. Time management begins with the creation of an agenda. Research shows that the faster the group proceeds through an agenda item the more satisfied the members feel and the more they perceive that the group is successful. With this in mind group leaders fractionalize major agenda items into smaller ones so they can be dispatched more quickly, leading to the desired feelings of success and satisfaction.

Proxemics

If you think about the rooms in which groups of which you were a member met you can recall various arrangements of furniture and objects. Also, you can visualize differences in the ways in which individuals space themselves with respect to the furniture and other individuals. Communication through the use and structuring of space is called *proxemic communication.*

We speak generally of *static space* and *dynamic space.* Static space communicates much about status. The size, location, and privacy of space communicates the rank of its occupant. Thus we find senior executives in spacious, top-floor, private chambers, while typists in a steno pool usually are housed below the top floor in cramped areas that are open to almost anyone who cares to enter. High-status people are found at the head of the table; lesser people on the sides. The whole *Dilbert* movement was spawned by the cubicle workspace.

Dynamic space is the personal area that each of us stakes out and protects as we move about. When strangers gather, for instance, they usually divide the available space. Thus, in a waiting area containing 15 chairs, five strangers usually sit so that two vacant chairs separate each person from the closest others. We can tolerate shrinkage of our personal space in crowds, for example, but as soon as possible we reestablish our territory. By allowing people to enter our personal space we communicate about our interpersonal relationships with them. In general the closer two individuals are to one another, the closer is their relationship.

Proxemics strategies can be used to manage the small group. For example, a group can be made to be more egalitarian by substituting a round table for a rectangular one. No one is at the head of the table. More recently the stand-up meeting has become popular. There are no chairs in the meeting room. McGinn (2000) reported that sit-down meetings last, on average, 34% longer than chair-free sessions. And, one of McGinn's interviewees reported, "We cover more material in a 15-minute stand-up meeting than you see covered in a two-hour sit-down meeting."

Objectics

If you think about the environments in which groups work, you may recall some of the objects in those environments. The effect of objects on communication is known as *objectics.* In a given room the furniture, paintings, carpet, and other objects suggest something about the activity that occurs in the room and about the occupants as well. Individuals often surround themselves with objects that are singularly revealing. We find such items as ashtrays, coffee cups, Phi Beta Kappa keys, briefcases, and so on.

Objects can communicate *status*, expensive homes, automobiles, watches, etc; *lifestyle,* skies, surfboards, musical instruments, books, etc; *sentimentality*, heirlooms, photos, children's possessions, etc; *values,* religious artifacts, cleaning products, food items, etc; and *goals,* pictures of houses hoped for, pictures of young children in cap and gown showing the goals for one's children, a picture of a retouched now slimmer person on the refrigerator door reminding the person of the consequences of overeating, etc.

Objects in small group and team meeting rooms are usually not numerous. There are some static ones, a picture on the wall of organizational founders and heroes perhaps, and maybe photos to motivate and show goals. A picture of a mountain suggests we must climb to the top, while an ocean photo may suggest no end to where we can go.

Summary

Presented in this chapter was information on ten categories of nonverbal communication and how these communication categories relate to group and team communication. Knowledge of nonverbal communication can help you become a better group and team communicator. And in a larger sense it can increase your awareness of and sensitivity to human interactions in any context. People watching, the most inexpensive entertainment, becomes ever so much more fascinating.

CHAPTER 6

LISTENING IN GROUPS AND TEAMS

Research suggests that listening occupies the largest portion of our total communication time. Barker et al. (1980), for example, reported that 40-70% of our communication time is spent on listening, 20-35% speaking, 10-20% reading, and 5-15% writing. In groups and teams the percentages are more heavily weighted to listening. For instance, in a group of three, if each member spoke an equal length of time, each member would be a listener 67% of the time. In a group of four each member would be a listener 75% of the time and in a group of five, each member would be a listener 80% of the time, again, providing speaking time were divided equally among the members. With the addition of each member to the group, listening time for every member of the group would increase.

We define *listening* as the reception and processing of messages. The receptive part is purely sensory and refers to the impingement of a physical stimulus on a sense organ. Sense organs then transmit their received information to the brain where the processing of the information is done.

Since we spend so much of our time listening one would think that listening is a desired activity because so many people are doing it for extended periods of time, particularly in groups. But that appears not to be the case. We might say with justification that there is a shortage of listeners, an assertion that could be supported by the large number of professional listeners, people who make their livelihood by listening. Psychotherapists of all schools are prime examples. In fact, orthodox psychoanalysts say virtually nothing in their sessions. Then there are *captive listeners*, people who are not paid directly for listening but who must do so nonetheless. Here we have the barbers, bartenders, hair stylists, people riding on airplanes, and so on. There are also the non-human listeners. Pets are such good listeners; they are non-judgmental. At the end of the day if you did not succeed at reaching your goals at work, if your house is a mess, and if you went off your diet, you can tell all this to your pet and your pet will still love you. One of the reasons why pets are such good therapists is that they are good, non-judgmental listeners.

Most everyone then is in search of a good listener, is in search of an audience. And subsequently in this chapter we will discuss the recruitment of listeners. But first the types of listening will be presented and discussed. Both *verbal listening* (listening to speech) and *nonverbal listening* (observing physical appearance, facial expressions, body movements and postures, touching, vocal characteristics, and time and space factors) will be discussed

Passive Listening

In *passive listening* you are just in the message environment and not dedicated to receiving any particular message. The messages are just part of the background. TV watching is often passive. You are there but you are not there. Some things are indeed learned during passive listening. TV commercials, for example, are at the same time irritating and memorable. We remember the jingles even though we never tried to do so. In groups similar things occur. You can attend only an initial group meeting and without any conscious intent you will be able to recognize the faces of the attendees at that initial meeting in another environment or at a subsequent meeting. This is an example of passive nonverbal listening.

Active Listening

In *active listening* there is a conscious intent to capture the information in a message so that it can be understood, remembered, recalled, and criticized. In active listening the listener must:

- *Focus* on the message. This means that the effects of any distractions must be minimized.
- *Understand* the message by trying to find the main points in the message and the support for these main points. Also, try to put everything in context. If a group meeting is about fund raising, for example, then this topic is one context. The group setting itself is another context. In any situation there are many contexts, physical, linguistic, nonverbal, social, interpersonal, cultural, and so on.
- *Remember* the message by making associations and using mnemonic devices. Memory experts who perform in clubs and on TV will hear and learn the names of 100 to 200 people at the beginning of a show, and then at the end of the show they will name these same people without a mistake. How do they do it? By associating names with faces. Mnemonic devices (memory techniques) include rhyme,

using the first letters of a word for each word in a string, and so on. The lead title of this book is easy to remember because of the rhyme. Acronyms, NATO, for example, use the first letter of each word to make a name.

- *Recall* the message so that you know for sure that you remember it and so that you can transmit it to someone else. Recalling and transmitting help to stabilize a message in memory. This notion is supported by the suggestion that if you want to learn something you should teach it.

- *Analyze* the message for the strengths and weaknesses of the information contained in the message.

As an overall example suppose that you are a member of a group learning how to perform cardio-pulmonary resuscitation (CPR) procedures. You must first begin to *focus* by eliminating distracting thoughts from your mind and asking that any environmental distractions (noise, for instance) be eliminated or attenuated. Next you must *understand* the information given by the trainer by tracking the trainer's main points and the support offered for these points. You must keep in mind context. One contextual factor is that you are learning about an emergency situation where time is of the essence; it is not a session on wine making. *Remembering* is your next step. You might find it useful to use a mnemonic device such as A-B-C. "A" is for clear the AIRWAY, "B" is for evoke the BREATHING response, and "C" is for facilitate CARDIAC functioning. Since CPR trainers use mannequins there are a host of nonverbal images that will facilitate the memory process as well. To *recall* and transmit you can use your experience of giving CPR to the mannequin, then repeat the process to show that you know it. This fits in with the description of medical training: "See one–do one–show one." Watch an appendectomy, then do an appendectomy, and then show someone else how to do an appendectomy. Finally after doing all of the above you can now *analyze* the CPR presentation. What were strengths and weaknesses. What changes would you make in the presentation to improve it?

Verbal and Nonverbal Listening

Generally verbal listening describes the listening you do when you hear speech. Speech is the carrier of information. Nonverbal listening, on the other hand, is most often concerned with socio-emotional factors. To be sure information can be transmitted nonverbally as it would be visually in a CPR demonstration, but over the long haul, nonverbal messages inform us about socio-emotional factors.

In a group or team as discussion proceeds you hear the words that are uttered and you listen to all the nonverbal messages surrounding those words. What is the tone of voice, the posture, the facial expression of the speaker, and so on? Do these nonverbal behaviors complement or contradict the speaker's verbal message? Any time someone speaks, the spoken words are imbedded in a sea of nonverbal behaviors. The astute listener listens not only to the words but observes the nonverbal behaviors surrounding those words.

One situation that demands that the nonverbal behaviors be listened to is the case in which you suspect that a speaker is lying, being deceptive, or spreading misinformation. The words will not reveal this but nonverbal behaviors might; the speaker may hesitate, be dysfluent, lose eye contact, engage in lip biting and lip licking, move a hand to the face, rock on one foot, and so on. These are some of the nonverbal behaviors that accompany lying.

The astute listener must not only listen to the person in the group who is speaking at the moment but must observe the group as a whole. This is so important when you enter a group. Often when you enter a group for the first time you feel like you have reached nirvana. But you know this is a mirage. You know there are coalitions, that some members do not like other members. What appears to be nirvana is often a minefield. If you become too friendly with persons A, B, and C, then persons D, E, and F will not like you. How do you get a grip on the situation? You do so by observing the nonverbal behaviors of the group members. Who sits with whom? Who frowns when someone speaks? Who arrives late when another person is scheduled to lead off the meeting? Who is occupied with personal paperwork when another speaks? Observing these and a plethora of other nonverbal behaviors will inform you about the socio-emotional make-up of the group.

At times the situation is quite striking. Let us suppose that a motion has been made and seconded and that it is to be discussed at the next meeting. But surprisingly at the next meeting a number of members are silent; they do not join the discussion. Silence is a key nonverbal message. What does the silence mean in this particular situation? Most likely it means that the decision has already been made, that someone was "politicking" between meetings and got a majority. The meeting is superfluous; the discussion is a sham; the fix was in.

Of course not all nonverbal messages are on the dark side. Cherished moments in groups can be revealed nonverbally. When a group achieves its goal, beats the competition, resolves a conflict amicably, it often exhibits celebratory nonverbal behaviors. And the astute nonverbal listener should be sensitive to these as well.

Indices of Listening

How can you show that you are listening and that you are an effective listener? There are a number of responses that reveal this:

- *Reflective Responses:* A reflective response paraphrases or parrots the speaker's utterance. <u>Speaker:</u> *I worked in Turkey before my transfer to Mozambique.* <u>Listener:</u> *I see. You worked in Turkey before Mozambique.*

- *Interpretive Responses:* Interpretive responses reveal that the listener has not responded to the face value of the speaker's utterance, but is interpreting it. **Speaker:** *My supervisor told me to speak up and give my opinions, and when I did, he fired me.* **Listener:** *You feel that your supervisor betrayed you.*

- *Clarifying Responses:* Clarifying responses are designed to bring clarity to the speaker's utterance. **Speaker:** *I can attend meetings on Tuesday and Thursdays but not all the time.* **Listener:** *Can you attend this Tuesday and Thursday?*

- *Empathic Responses:* Empathic responses indicate that you are responding to the speaker's feelings. **Speaker:** *I apologize for being inadequately prepared today.* **Listener:** *I understand, I know the shape I was in when we had our first child.*

The above listening responses show not only that a listener is listening but they extend some sensitivity to the speaker as well. There is no belittling of the speaker and no negative criticism is presented. There is a time for criticism, but first listeners must fully understand the speaker's message and this can only be done by listening. Finally, it is clear that the above listening responses are primarily verbal. There are, however, nonverbal indices of listening as well.

Included in the repertoire of nonverbal listening responses during verbal interaction are the head nod, eye contact, and the "Mm hms" and "Uh huhs." We call these behaviors *communication lubricants;* they "grease" the interaction and are the little tidbits of communication that are so innocuous and meaningless, but communication interaction would wither and die without them.

Recruiting Listeners

We all need listeners. There are *psychological* reasons underlying this need. Psychologically when someone listens to you, you feel that someone cares, that you are not alone, and that you are someone of value. Just the presence of the listener can be comforting. The orthodox psychoanalyst (one who strictly adheres to the principles of Freud) who says virtually nothing during a session and who avoids face-to-face contact with the patient, still evokes verbal output from the patient. All of us to one degree or another serve as therapists when we graciously and non-judgmentally listen to others. And all of us to some extent play the role of counseling clients when others in turn listen to us graciously and non-judgmentally. When we talk and someone listens graciously and non-judgmentally we can experience *catharsis,* the state of feeling relieved after verbalizing. Catharsis seems to occur because verbalization reduces stress, it takes a "load off our shoulders," and it produces new perceptions that lead to greater insights about self and others.

Listeners satisfy other psychological needs as well. For example, there is a need to lead, to exert power, and to control. These are sometimes referred to as *ego* needs. In a group the person who speaks at length; does not permit interruptions; who gives information, suggestions, and opinions; and who does not ask for information, suggestions, and opinions is usually the power person in the group. This person is the member other members listen to and the attention given is quite rewarding and ego boosting.

The above discussion supports the assertion that there are psychological benefits in having someone listen to you. To experience these benefits you must find or recruit listeners. How do you do this? Somehow you must *empower* yourself. This you can do by improving your social skills. By improving your personal appearance, by moving to a new location, by taking risks, by joining social groups and improvement classes, and by improving your communication skills. Tom Peters (1993) had empowerment in mind when he said that your skills should be better and your network richer at the end of this year than they were at the beginning.

Summary

The largest proportion of our communication time is spent listening. We all have a need for listeners and much time, effort, and money is spent to satisfy this need. Listening can be active or passive and it can be verbal or nonverbal. There are a number of categories of listening responses that can be used in learning to be an effective listener.

CHAPTER 7

THEORIES OF GROUP DEVELOPMENT

Systems Theory

A *system* is a set of interdependent parts or elements that form a whole and work together to achieve a goal. A simple system, for example, would be the heating and cooling system familiar to many. A heating and cooling system has three basic parts or elements: a *sensor*, a *comparator*, and an *activator*. The sensor senses the temperature in a room and communicates the room's temperature to the comparator which compares the actual room temperature (provided by the sensor) to the desired temperature communicated by the room's occupant when the occupant set the thermostat. If there is a match (usually within plus or minus five degrees is considered a match), the system does nothing. If there is no match, the system calls on the activator to create a match. If the occupant of the room wants a temperature of 75 degrees and the room is actually 67 degrees the activator generates heat; if the room were 81 degrees the activator would kick in the cooling system. All this activity is designed to have the system achieve its goal which, in this case, is to maintain a room temperature of 75 degrees.

Systems Concepts

Closed or Open

A system can be closed or open. A *closed* system is one that is not receiving energy from the environment; it is dying. A mechanical watch "dies" if it is never rewound or never receives energy from the environment. A dying star collapses into itself and never shines again. Our concern will be with *open* systems, systems that receive energy from the environment. Our simple heating and cooling system discussed above is open, being energized by electricity.

Interdependence of Parts or Elements

The parts or elements of a system are interdependent. None can be removed or disabled without disabling the entire system. A heating and cooling system with an inoperative sensor could suffer a system meltdown, since the remaining components of the system might endlessly produce heat or cold because a vital message, actual room temperature, would never be received.

Hierarchy

Even though there is an interdependence among its parts or components, in some systems some parts are more important than others. An example is the human body. If the body suffers traumatic injury, the brain will horde the remaining blood for itself, shutting off the supply to the extremities. This fact of nature is understandable for if the brain dies so does the rest of the body.

Feedback

All systems have inter-component communication. In our heating and cooling system the sensor communicates to the comparator which communicates to the activator which may or may not take action. If the activator does begin to heat and cool, the sensor feeds back to the system the results of the activator's efforts in order to inform the activator to stop or to keep going.

Equilibrium

All systems strive to reach a goal. When a system reaches its goal we say that the system is in *equilibrium*. Equilibrium is a very important systems concept since it marks the attainment of the goal state of the system. All system efforts are designed to reach equilibrium. When our heating and cooling system has produced a room temperature of 75 degrees, the system has achieved a state of equilibrium and will remain in that stage until the temperature deviates by a fixed amount from 75 (plus or minus five degrees). Then the system falls into a state of *disequilibrium* and once again the activator must be engaged.

Groups As Systems

Researchers and scholars have found it useful to apply Systems Theory to groups and teams. In this conceptualization group members are the components in the system, the system is open since members receive physical energy (food, air, and water) and non-physical energy (social support, information, and resources) from the environment, and group members are interdependent. There is often a system hierarchy since some members appear to be more important than others, there is feedback or communication between and among members, and all groups strive to achieve equilibrium, i.e., they strive to reach their goal.

Unlike physical systems, in which system components are connected physically by wires or electromagnetic waves, for example, in groups the connections for message transmission are sensual media, air for the transmission of visual, auditory, and olfactory images, skin for the transmission of touch, and the tongue for the transmission of gustatory stimuli. Of course there are often physical interfaces in group telephony or in computer-mediated communication.

Group Development Theories

We will now consider a number of group development theories that are anchored to Systems Theory.

Lewin's Field Theory

Lewin (1948) was concerned with *physical* and *psychological* space. He noted that at any moment it is possible to be situated in a given physical space but, at the same time, to be travelling widely in psychological space. For example, give yourself a little test. Think of all the times your mind drifted in the last 30 minutes. Where did you go? Whom did you see and talk to? Did you fantasize? Yes, it is possible indeed to travel in your mind in psychological space while sitting in one physical location. Drifting off, thinking about other things can be a result of boredom, fatigue, worry, distractions, associations, and, in many cases, simply wanting to be in the place about which you are thinking.

Lewin believed that a group is in a state of equilibrium when the members' physical and psychological spaces coincide. This means that the group members are in the same physical location and they are in the same psychological location which is identical to the physical. Group members are together and they want to be together. Groups often begin in a state of equilibrium, but interpersonal conflict often arises, causing members to drift off into different psychological spaces even though they are physically together. This is a state of disequilibrium. Task difficulty, too, can cause disequilibrium. A group can have harmonious interpersonal relations but if they repeatedly fail to solve the problem assigned to them, they might go into a state of disequilibrium. Outside forces can also cause disequilibrium. A group that is in a state of equilibrium might go into a state of disequilibrium if its funding were terminated, for example. But, if the group is to be successful, it must eventually reach a state of equilibrium once again.

Bennis and Shepard

Bennis and Shepard (1956) looked at issues of *authority* and *intimacy* in the group with respect to group development.

In a group just formed there is often a state of equilibrium with respect to authority but this state is short-lived. Soon aggressive members begin to dominate. This is called the *dependence-submission phase* of development. Next is a reaction to the aggressive members and the group is restructured. This is the stage of *counter-dependence*. Finally there is the *resolution stage*. Here the power struggle is over and a state of equilibrium with respect to power and authority is achieved. The group "gets down to business." The group becomes a group.

Bennis and Shepard believe that interpersonal relationships in the group follow a developmental pattern. In the beginning there is a period of happiness, much talking and laughing. This is the stage of *enchantment*, but soon conflict emerges and people are not getting along. This is the stage of *disenchantment*. Eventually group members realize that if they are to be successful in their task they must get along and work as a group. This is the *consensual validation* stage and in this stage equilibrium is achieved.

Mintzberg, Raisinghani, and Theoret

Mintzberg, Raisinghani, and Theoret (1976) focus on the problem-solving process. In the beginning a group can be in a state of equilibrium, but then a problem is identified or discovered. This throws the group into a state of disequilibrium. There is conflict, not interpersonal conflict, but conflict with the problem. It is the group versus the problem. Mintzberg, Raisinghani, and Theoret propose a three-stage developmental model. In Stage 1, the problem *identification* stage, the problem is recognized. In this stage activity toward solving the problem is evoked, obstacles to solving the problem are recognized, and possible cause-effect relations underlying the problem are examined.

In Stage 2, the *solution* stage, activities leading to the development of one or more solutions are triggered. First the group determines if there are any ready-made solutions. For example, think of all the computer programs already written. If you want to do any number of statistical operations you do not have to start from scratch and write the program. That problem has already been solved. Therefore, many problems have already been solved so the first step in problem solving is to see if a solution already exists. Searching for, finding, and using a ready-made solution is called the *algorithmic* approach.

For many problems, however, there are no ready-made solutions. We do not have sufficient information nor can we obtain it. Or, there may be so much information that we have no way of analyzing it. We must rely on hunches, insights, rules of thumb, and do the best we can with what we have. This we call the *heuristic* approach to problem solving. Heuristic solutions are designed and usually result from extensive group interaction.

Stage 3 of the Mintzberg, Raisinghani, and Theoret theory is called *selection*. In this stage possible solutions are screened to reduce their number, the remaining solutions are evaluated, and one is selected and ratified by the group. Once the selected solution is ratified group equilibrium is restored and will remain so until the next problem is identified.

Tuckman

Tuckman (1965) saw four stages of group development: forming, storming, norming, performing.

In Stage 1, *forming*, group members are concerned with orientation matters. Members try to find the boundaries of the group by testing. What are the behavioral limits? In addition, members think about leadership and followership and who will fill these roles. In general the climate is affable and the group is in equilibrium.

In Stage 2, *storming*, interpersonal conflict emerges. Group members may be upset with the mere fact that they are tied to a group. They may dislike the people who emerge as leaders or they may feel the approach to the task is all wrong. The interpersonal conflict does affect task accomplishment for if two members dislike each other, they will tend to criticize each other's ideas as well.

In Tuckman's Stage 3, *norming*, ingroup feeling and cohesiveness develop, new group roles and rules evolve and are adopted, and group members are more open in their expressions of opinion. The group begins to operate as a group.

Finally, in Tuckman's Stage 4, *performing*, the group's interpersonal conflicts are resolved. This allows the group to focus its energy on the task and its completion. Equilibrium is achieved.

Fisher

Very much parallel to Tuckman's theory is the theory of Fisher (1970). Again four stages are proposed. In the first, *orientation*, members get acquainted, tentatively express their attitudes, and generally create a positive social-emotional climate. The group is in equilibrium. Next, in Stage 2, *conflict* emerges and members express negative attitudes, there is disagreement, and coalitions form. In Stage 3, the *emergence* stage, conflicts are reduced. Finally in Stage 4, the *reinforcement* stage, decisions are made, endorsed, and reinforced by the members. Equilibrium is established.

Bales and Strodtbeck

Bales and Strodbeck (1951) found three distinct phases that groups go through as they proceed toward their goals: 1) emphasis on problems of orientation, 2) emphasis on problems of evaluation, and 3) emphasis on problems of control. In Phase 1, group members would be involved in exchanging information; in Phase 2, the expression of opinions, evaluations, and feelings emerge; and in Phase 3, group members suggest possible courses of action.

Bales and Strodtbeck found that all along the way group members would keep a balance between task and socio-emotional utterances thereby supporting Bales' (1950) notion that there always must be a balance between the two if a group is to survive and be productive. Moreover, the researchers found that once a group makes a decision the number of negative utterances usually falls off and the number of positive utterances rises sharply.

Bales and Strodtbeck provided one of the first reports on group development and influenced a number of researchers who followed them, notably Fisher and Tuckman.

Discussion

Observers of the groups that generated data for the above theories have noted that communication seems to peak at the beginning and end of the respective developmental sequences. Thus, communication peaks at equilibrium states and is reduced when the groups are in states of disequilibrium caused by interpersonal conflict or conflict with the challenges posed by the problem or task. A group meeting for an extended period of time can cycle and recycle through the stages of the various theories. Whether recycling is a help or hindrance to good group performance is not known. It is possible for a group to skip a stage. One might imagine a group that simply does not experience conflict. Finally, the stages described in the theories have some relationship to the stages of a drama. First, there is the setting, time and place, for example, of the play and the introduction of the characters. Next, there is conflict. And finally, there is conflict resolution, either a tragic resolution (tragedy) or a happy one (comedy). This general outline is followed whether the presentation is a 30-minute TV sitcom, a Shakespearean drama, or a group or team working on a problem.

Summary

In this chapter we first looked at Systems Theory and the concepts related to that general theory. Next, group developmental theories were examined. Each of the theories examined was Systems Theory based. In particular each theory looked at groups as passing through states of equilibrium and disequilibrium.

CHAPTER 8

FORMING

In this chapter we will discuss group formation. In particular we will explore the reasons for people joining groups, and, then, we will examine group dynamics as groups form and members begin to interact.

Why Do People Join Groups?

Biological Reasons

We join groups because we are biologically "wired up" to do so. Group formations are genetically determined. This argument is reviewed by

Bower (1995a, 1995b) who notes that just as a bee is part of a larger group, the hive, and cannot survive alone, so is an individual genetically wired to be part of a group. Bower, in this vein, quotes David Sloan Wilson who defines a group as consisting:

> simply of a set of individuals influenced by the expression of an inherited trait, even if the group assembles intermittently and some of its members leave or enter at various times (Bower, 1995a, p. 328).

Some individuals have stronger "group genes" than others. This is why some groups survive and others do not. One such genetic trait is the altruistic trait, the tendency for an organism to sacrifice itself for the common good of the group. There is some evidence to suggest that groups of altruists survive longer than groups of self-serving members. A second genetic trait seems to be the ability some individuals have to quickly and correctly spot cooperative individuals, non-cooperative individuals, and cheaters. Bower cites evidence that supports this notion. After 30 minutes of social interaction group members predicted with substantial accuracy which of the group members were most likely to behave selfishly in a prisoner's dilemma game. A third genetic trait is related to group decision making. It seems that just as there are genetically-determined decision-making behaviors in the beehive, so does human decision making have a genetic basis. Finally, it may be possible that all of us are, as individuals, just partial people. Only by joining the group is our genetic potential realized. The whole or group is indeed greater than the sum of the parts or the individuals that comprise it.

In sum, those who argue that we join groups because we are biologically wired up to do so take a very deterministic position. Like lions that are wired up to live in prides, fish that are wired up to live in schools, birds that are wired up to live in flocks, we too are wired up to live in groups. And if we have good group genes our survival chances are enhanced.

Interpersonal Reasons

Another perspective on the "Why do we join groups?" question is that the group experience is necessary to satisfy key interpersonal needs. Theorists who argue from this perspective are Schutz, Maslow, and Goffman.

Schutz's Interpersonal Needs Theory

According to Schutz (1966) every individual has three interpersonal needs that can be satisfied only through the group experience. They are *inclusion*, *control*, and *affection*.

Inclusion

Inclusion refers to the need to be in a group. At the *feeling* level, this need is satisfied if a person desires the company of others and is interested in others. Inclusion at the *behavioral* level is satisfied when the individual actually is in a group and is included and accepted by other group members. To force oneself into a group does not completely satisfy the inclusion need. The other group members must accept your presence and be interested in you. The inclusion need can be shown to be unsatisfied whenever there is too much or too little inclusive behavior. The person who joins every group, attends every party, and so on is exhibiting apprehension in the inclusion area. The same apprehension is exhibited by the person who goes nowhere, joins no club and remains a recluse. In different ways both individuals show a failure in satisfying the need for inclusion.

In terms of self-concept, the people who satisfy their inclusion needs have a feeling that they are significant, that they are wanted by others and that they are missed from group meetings when they are absent. Those who fail to satisfy this need have the feeling that they are insignificant, that they are "nobodies."

In extreme cases, failure to satisfy the inclusion need can lead to psychosis or schizophrenia, wherein the individual apparently is included only in his created inner world of fantasies and delusions. Schutz has said for all interpersonal needs, for instance:

> Non-fulfillment of an interpersonal need leads to mental illness and sometimes death. Unsatisfactory personal relations lead directly to difficulties associated with emotional illness. Death, either through suicide or resulting from the more general loss of motivation for life, results when interpersonal dissatisfaction is prolonged.

Control

The need for control refers to the need to be respected by others for our competence, skills, and leadership ability, and the need to respect the same control qualities in others. At the *feeling* level, people are able to lead others because of their leadership skills or because of their demonstrated skills and competencies.

The need for control like the need for inclusion, is satisfied in a group at some "happy medium." The person who tries to dominate everyone and who tries to be the best at everything is communicating apprehension about satisfying the control need. This person Schutz labeled the *autocrat*. A person, behaving quite differently, can nonetheless show an equal failure at satisfying the control need. This person is submissive, is dominated, and is the one Schutz labels an *abdicrat*. The person who successfully satisfies the control need Schutz labeled a *democrat*.

With respect to self-concept, people who have satisfied the control need are those who feel responsible and competent, who can respect the skill and competencies of others, and who can lead as well as follow. These are the *true democrats*. Not satisfying the control need leads to feelings of incompetence, indecisiveness, and irresponsibility. At the extremes, people who have not been successful in satisfying the control need may become obsessive-compulsive, manifest in ritualistically controlling the minutiae of everyday life, a baked potato must be pierced three times with a fork not two or four, for example; or they may turn inward again to a world of fantasy and delusion.

Affection

The need for affection includes the need to love and to be loved. At the *feeling* level, an individual likes or loves others. At the *behavioral* level, this love is reciprocally expressed. When it is behaviorally expressed, individuals become emotionally close. In the affection stage, there is the highest level of disclosure between individuals.

Implications of Schutz's Theory

Implied by Schutz's theory is a hierarchy. To reach the affection stage, one needs to satisfy the inclusion and control needs, and to satisfy the control need, one needs to first satisfy the inclusion need. Schutz referred to the inclusion need as the "in and out" need. To begin any relationship, one must first be included with at least one other person, preferably more than one, or a group.

Less evident is the dependence of affection on control. According to Schutz's theory, to be a person deserving affection, one must first feel competent, be competent, and be perceived as competent. One needs to have some skill to be lovable What can you do better than others? For what can you be admired? Just as it is essentially impossible to love a disembodied person, so it is almost equally difficult to love a person with absolutely no competencies or skills. The skills may be quite minor; it may be that a person can make better chip dip than anyone else. At least this represents some control. Employment is very much tied to the control need, for through our jobs we tell others of our competencies. It is not surprising, therefore, that layoffs and job losses can place great stress on relationships.

Assessing Interpersonal Needs

To assess the three interpersonal needs, Schutz constructed a test called FIRO-B (Fundamental Interpersonal Relations Orientation, Form B). The test taker answers 54 questions about feelings ("I like to...." questions) and behaviors ("I try to...." questions). Results of the test reveal where one stands in satisfying the three needs, at both the feeling and the behavioral levels. It can be used in any pre-post situation, that is, in a situation in which the test is given both before and after an event or intervention; counseling might be one example of such an event or intervention. Of course, like any test, the results are not ironclad, chiseled-in-stone truth, but must be interpreted in light of reliability and validity factors.

Maslow's Need Hierarchy

Maslow (1970) has postulated that all humans have certain needs that must be satisfied if we are to become self-actualized persons. Like Schutz's, Maslow's needs are arranged in a hierarchy, meaning lower level needs must be satisfied before the higher level needs can be satisfied. Maslow's needs and their meaning are:

- The *Physiological Need* refers to the need for air, water, and food.
- The *Safety Need* refers to the need to be sheltered from harm and assault.
- The *Belongingness Need* refers to people's need to feel that they are part of some group. Recall from Chapter 1 Erickson's model which noted that at every stage in life there is a primary group that contributes to our feeling of belonging.
- The *Esteem Need* refers to the need to be valued by others. Again this is a need satisfied primarily by the group.
- The *Self-Actualization Need* refers to the need to be all that you can be, a phrase co-opted by military recruiters. Self-actualized individuals

have reached a level of independence and autonomy. They are somewhat immune from everyday controversies.

According to Maslow, then, if we are to satisfy the needs of life, group
interaction is necessary. This provides another answer to the question,
"Why do people join groups?"

Goffman's Need to Impress View

The most pervasive human need is to impress others.

For Goffman, (1959, 1963) impressing others is the primary need. He
would disagree with Maslow who puts physiological and safety needs first.
Goffman notes that people will chance the loss of life and limb to impress
others. There are the daredevils, high wire walkers, motorcycle stunt drivers, sky divers, bungee jumpers, and binge drinkers, for example. These are
blatant examples. Less obvious are those who sleep too little, smoke, eat
and drink too much; those who exhibit Type A behaviors; and those in general who abuse their health. Why? They are driven to succeed, to impress.

To impress you must have an audience, of course, and this is where
groups come in. Few of us stand before a large crowd and communicate
live and few of us communicate to a large audience via television. For the
vast majority of people the audience is a small group be it a social group or
a task group. The need to impress is satisfied primarily in the group.

One might argue with the extremeness of Goffman's view. Indeed it was
noted that Goffman's view stands in contrast to Maslow's. At the same
time, is it wrong to want to impress? It depends. If we look again at the
views of Schutz and Maslow we will see that people must satisfy the need
to control, and Maslow notes that people must satisfy the need for esteem
if higher order needs are to be satisfied. For people to satisfy the respective
control and esteem needs mandates that they impress others. Therefore,

impressing others seems to be necessary. If the need to impress becomes an obsession, however, then it may become counterproductive to both the individual and the group.

In sum, according to Goffman, we join groups so that we have available audiences to impress.

Practical Reasons for Joining Group

There are, of course, practical reasons for people joining groups.

- Some things we cannot do by ourselves. We cannot move a piano up a staircase by ourselves, for example.

- We join groups because we are interested in certain activities that are group defined. If we are interested in playing softball, for example, we are locked in to a group activity.

- We may join a group because our personal goals can only be realized through group membership. To improve the quality of life in their town may require citizens to join a civic activist group, for instance.

- We join groups because we are required to do so. In most task groups members have been assigned to the group as part of their employment. There are an endless list of committees and teams to which one can be assigned.

Dynamics Of The Newly Formed Group

In the newly formed group there is usually a high level of affability, friendliness, and in general, a very positive interpersonal climate. This climate is interpreted differently by three types of group members.

The Naïve Member

The *naïve* member believes that the positive interpersonal climate of the newly formed group is real, that this is the way these people really are, and that the group experience will be very rewarding.

The Sophisticated Member

The *sophisticated* group member will know that the interpersonal climate in the first meeting is not real, that group members are really sizing up one another. The sophisticated member is trying to determine who will lead, who will follow, who will cooperate, and who will be operating from a position of self-interest. The sophisticated member's surveillance of the group is done for the benefit of the group. The sophisticated member is dedicated to having the group succeed.

The Game Player

The *game player* is very affable and knows that his or her affability and the affability of others is not real. But, unlike the sophisticated member, the game player's surveillance of the group is done for selfish reasons. Game players are thinking about which members can be exploited, which members can be recruited to advance the game player's agendas, and which members can be deceived. All this they are thinking as they are being friendly and affable. Naïve members are seen as easy prey by game players.

Common hidden agendas of game players are to control the group, to take credit for the ideas generated by the group, and to change the direction of the group or alter the group's goal, all for self-promotion and advancement.

Overall then, on the surface, the early or formation session of a group is usually friendly and affable. But this interpersonal climate is superficial.

While people are friendly, they are also sizing up one another, thinking about who will lead, who will follow, who will cooperate, who will operate from pure self-interest, and so on.

Summary

There are four major reasons for people joining groups: biological, interpersonal, actualizational, and need to impress. Writers who proposed the four reasons are respectively Bower, Schutz, Maslow, and Goffman. In any newly formed group certain roles emerge. Included are the naïve, sophisticated, and game-playing roles.

CHAPTER 9

STORMING

Storming refers to the conflict phase of group development. In Tuckman's organizational scheme, this is Stage 2. After forming, Stage 1 groups often go through a conflict phase before getting down to business. It is possible for conflict to emerge at any time, of course, but researchers have noted a consistency of its occurrence after the forming stage. *Conflict* refers to the anxiety generated when a choice between or among alternatives must be made. Many conflicts are benign and of little consequence: should you order the special of the day or should you order your usual selection; should you go to this film or that film; or should you vacation at the beach or in the mountains? Of course, some people experience anguish even over making these simple, inconsequential decisions. Other decisions are more worrisome: should you complain to a superior about a work or school situation that you believe is wrong or unjust even if your complaint leads to your being suspended or censured; should you change your life style to care for an elderly parent; or should you marry or divorce? These are more serious conflicts. Needless to say, we all experience conflict; we simply cannot avoid it. What we can try to do is to limit the damaging effects of conflict and to capitalize on any positive effects of conflict whenever possible.

Types of Conflict in Groups and Teams

The types of conflict of importance in small group and team communication are personal, interpersonal, task, and administrative.

Personal Conflict

Even though it is confined within a single group member, *personal conflict* can nonetheless affect the group. One of the most common forms of personal conflict concerns joining or not joining the group in the first place. Suppose you are asked to join a group. This invitation can generate conflict for, on one hand, you see possible benefit in joining, benefits like companionship; positive feedback that would enhance your self-concept; and increasing the number of people in your network, people who might help you in the future, for example. On the other hand, you might have had negative group experiences in the past; people did not show up for meetings when they said they would; group members were selfish, touting the group's ideas as their own; or coalitions formed in the group and the experience was always a case of us against them, for instance. These past experiences most likely would force you into a quandary, leading you to ask yourself, "Should I join or not?" The conflict intensifies if a superior asks or orders you to join a group or team. Here there is a fear of serious reprisal if you do not.

Interpersonal Conflict

Interpersonal conflict occurs when one group member has a negative emotional reaction toward another group member's behaviors and must decide to accept those behaviors or to confront the offending member. Again, a member in such a situation of interpersonal conflict must think of the consequences, keeping in mind that those consequences can be serious and long-lasting. Certain people like to dominate, and when two or more dominators are in the same group, there is usually a power struggle. Group members often resent members who do not carry their share of the load. Coalitions often form and solidify and members of the blue team and the red team resent each other. Romance sometimes develops even in a task group and often group members resent the distractions that can be generated by the romantic couple. And, the group's goals become secondary to the romantic couple who pursue their romantic impulses and ignore the group's needs.

Task Conflict

Task Conflict occurs when the group cannot decide between or among strategic alternatives. Suppose a group is given the task of developing a plan to lower the degree of voter apathy. Voter apathy has been defined for the group as less than 55% of eligible voters voting. As possible solutions are generated and discussed, a number of alternative strategies for the group to follow will be revealed. Some members will want to begin with surveys and focus groups; in short, these members believe that the best first step is to talk to the voters. Other members may feel that they know why voter apathy exists and feel that surveys and focus groups are a waste of time and money. These members may feel that the election process excludes certain people from participating because of lack of funds, for example. Therefore, to these members, the solution should begin with restructuring the whole election process. It may be possible to incorporate all alternative strategies into a proposed solution, but this is seldom possible because of the limits on available time, money, and resources, and because alternative solutions may conflict with or contradict one another.

The intensity with which one group member proposes and defends a solution, and the intensity with which a member criticizes the ideas of others can turn task conflict into interpersonal conflict. When the intensities are great, task conflict often does turn into interpersonal conflict. For example, for a dominating group member, it is not enough to propose a strategy and explain it. The personality of the dominator requires that all members endorse the proposed idea. If they do not offer their endorsement, the dominator becomes angry and interpersonal conflict emerges.

Often what appears to be task conflict is really masked interpersonal conflict. For example, if a group member does not like you, the chances are high that any idea or suggestion you make in the group will be criticized, not because of the merits of your suggestion, but simply because of the animosity that the member holds toward you.

Administrative Conflict

Administrative conflict arises over disagreements over plans and procedures needed to guide the group to task completion. Here the concern is with schedules, agendas, timelines, personnel assignments, and so on. Underlying almost all administrative conflicts is the fact that virtually everyone has a very crowded schedule. This is true not only of adults but of children as well. Finding a time to meet, therefore, is very difficult. Most imperative for any newly-constituted group is to find a common time at which everyone can regularly meet and then have each member block out that time and commit to it. This is so important because when the common time is established and there is absenteeism, most likely the absenteeism is symptomatic of another problem, usually interpersonal conflict. Having an established time for regular meetings is advantageous also because it in itself saves a tremendous amount of time. Some groups spend an unbelievable amount of time trying to find a time for the next meeting, with members sitting around with their personal calendars and electronic personal assistants like bingo players looking at their cards after each call to see if they have won.

Group Management of Conflict

Force

Although it is seldom pleasant and often not fair, conflict can be ended by the sheer use of power. A powerful group leader can simply dismiss a dissenting member, thereby ending conflict in a group at least temporarily. Rarely is physical force used in a task group; indeed, if it is, it is usually a sign of group disintegration. But power and status are the symbolic equivalents of physical force. Tom Siebel (Warner, 2000), CEO of Siebel Systems, for example, demands that all employees who have contact with customers dress in a specified way, men in crisp suits and ties and women in skirted suits or pantsuits with pantyhose, dress requirements unusual for a Silicon Valley company. There are no conflicts, no discussions about these requirements. If an employee disagrees with them the employee is no longer at Siebel.

Majority Vote

There is good reason why so many deliberative bodies, legislative, electoral boards, committees, small groups, teams, and so on use *majority vote* to make decisions. It is quick and, therefore, a time saver. Besides ending discussion, majority vote also can end conflict, providing the losing side or sides accept the decision of the vote. The acceptance is not always forthcoming. At times, say in a five to four vote, four members in a group of nine might be very unhappy. This unhappiness can damage group harmony, a rupture that may or may not be healed. It behooves the majority members to be humble in victory and to extend the olive branch to the minority. This will serve to preserve group harmony and will lessen the harboring of feelings of revenge by the minority. Voting decisions tend to be more extreme than decisions reached by other methods because a single point of view predominates.

Negotiation

In *negotiation*, everyone wins a little and loses a little. Because everyone wins something, disappointment and anger are minimized or eliminated and conflict itself, therefore, is minimized or eliminated. Suppose you are appointed to a civic committee formed to find ways to attract tourists to your hometown. The committee is given a travel budget allocated for the purpose of having committee members travel to towns that are comparable to yours and have good tourist businesses. The chair of the committee suggests that travel funds be used only by committee officers, chair, vice chair, and recording secretary. You disagree. Can you negotiate? Well, first you must have something to give if you are to get. This is a requirement in negotiation. What you can give, for example, is your promise to vote with the chair on some future vote, particularly a vote that will be expected to be close. You will give this vote in exchange for "your share" of the travel funds. In large and small deliberative bodies, vote trading is one of the most common currencies of negotiation. The process can be time consuming.

Negotiated agreements are often patchwork agreements. They often make little sense. In the U.S. Congress, they are often referred to as "pork barrel" agreements, something in the barrel for almost every congressional district. Thus a school lunch program bill may contain provisions for a waterway in one state, a bridge in another, an airport in a third, and so on. Groups that reach agreement through negotiation may not be cohesive groups but, at the same time, group members feel some satisfaction in reaching an agreement, winning something, and not losing too much.

Consensus

In *consensus* building, conflict is reduced by having group members agree upon a course of action before a decision is made. Like negotiation, this is a time-consuming process, and by the time an agreement is developed among all group members, the solution might be rather "watered down." Former British Prime Minister Margaret Thatcher depicted consensus in a stinging criticism.

> The process of abandoning all beliefs, principles, values and policies in search of something in which no one believes, but to which no one objects; the process of avoiding the very issues that may have to be solved, merely because you cannot get agreement on the way ahead. What great cause would have been fought and won under the banner, "I stand for consensus"? (See Will, 1977)

Nonetheless, when a decision comes about as a result of everyone's cooperation and every group member agrees on the decision, group harmony emerges. This harmony can be the trade-off for a decision that indeed may be watered down.

As was already mentioned, consensus building is time consuming. Consensus builders are sometimes said to have their *MBWA* (Management By Walking Around) degrees. What is meant by this is that they spend a large proportion of their working hours talking to group members or employees trying to find a consensus on a particular issue. In a factory it might be how to improve productivity 3%, or in a small group, say a job search committee, how to build a consensus around one job candidate. At times our MBWA person uses persuasion to subtly promote a particular position, but most of the time the person is a data gatherer, trying to find the positions on issues that group members hold in common.

Mediation

In *mediation*, conflicts are solved by bringing in a disinterested third party. The third party can be one person or several. If several, an odd number must be on the mediation team so that a tie vote can be broken should a vote be needed. Key to the selection of the third party is the participation of the conflicting parties. If there is one mediator, both conflicting parties must agree on that person. If multiple mediators are selected, say three, each conflicting party would pick one, and the chosen two would pick the third, or the two conflicting parties would agree on the third. Mediated decisions are non-binding.

Arbitration

In terms of procedures, *arbitration* is identical to mediation, that is, the arbitrator or arbitrators are selected by both conflicting parties. The only difference is that an arbitration decision is binding. Both conflicting parties must accept it. A good mediator or arbitrator must be a person of high credibility, trustworthiness, and expertise.

Fractionalization

Fractionalization is a method that can reduce or resolve conflict because it allows the group to experience success. In fractionalization, the group or group leader breaks a large task into a series of smaller tasks. Each component task is easier to contemplate and complete than the whole. Therefore, the group can experience success sooner and more often. Achieving success can reduce conflict; group members feel better about each other and themselves when they succeed. In this way both task and interpersonal conflict can be ameliorated. Fractionalization can also reduce administrative conflict. For example, in constructing an agenda for a meeting, fractionalization of the items into smaller items can allow the group to experience a series of successes sooner and more frequently. The group can feel that it is progressing: "Look how many agenda items we covered!"

The Personal Management of Conflict

There are some things an individual can do to help manage conflict in a group. Some suggestions that you might find helpful are:

Use the "Count to Ten" Rule

Conflict in a group is felt. We do not need to be told that we are in conflict. We feel it, and that feeling reflexively prompts us to recoil and to attack. This is a natural reaction. Nonetheless, we should try to use the "*Count to Ten*" Rule. The message in this homespun aphorism is simply think before acting. When in conflict, before saying or doing anything, count to ten. Impulsive emotional reactions are often regretted. Such reactions may antagonize another member and create an unresolved interpersonal conflict. And once bridges are burned, there is no turning back.

Introspect

When you get that feeling of conflict, think about why you feel the way you feel. This is *introspection*. Are your feelings justified? For example, if another group member presented an idea that was superior to yours, anger about this may be unjustified. If, on the other hand, another group member misrepresented and distorted your idea then a response from you is justified. Just how you might respond is discussed in the next section.

Depersonalize Your Comments

When expressing disagreement with a suggestion or opinion, do it tactfully. Separate suggestions and opinions from their offerers. Instead of referring to "John's idea" you might refer to "the idea on the table." Never use loaded words like "Your idea stinks," for example. This only creates antagonism. Face saving is important, that is, group members should not feel that they are being attacked and that they must defend themselves. Fractionalize your comments. If you are commenting on an idea just offered you might comment on the positive aspects of the idea and then talk about the areas where you have questions. Often when you tactfully ask questions about an idea the person who offered the idea will be open to modifying it.

The group's task or goal must be kept in mind at all times. Communication in the group should be tailored to having the group complete the task or meet the goal. At all times you must insist that you be respected. At times courtesy, civility, and kindness are mistaken for weakness, and other group members may feel that they can "walk all over you" if you are kind and courteous. Do not allow this to happen. Simply insist on being treated with respect.

Listen Attentively

Careful listening can attenuate conflict for it allows you to analyze proposed ideas and solutions very carefully. If you listen carefully you know exactly what was said and can discuss the ideas more intelligently. Moreover, knowing what was said in the course of a discussion can help you build on what was said and integrate it into a more robust idea or solution. Suggestions for effective listening were presented in an earlier chapter.

Don't Be Defensive

If your ideas and suggestions are rejected, do not take it as personal rejection. No one likes to lose, but remember that you are in a group. If your ideas and suggestions were not accepted, keep in mind that your rejected ideas quite possibly strengthened the ideas that eventually emerged. And always remember there will be another day.

Be Cooperative

If your ideas and suggestions have been rejected, go along with the decision. Let the group members know that you will support them. You may feel that you didn't argue your points as well as you might have during the discussion period, but you can think about this in terms of future discussions. Indeed, you can inform the group that you feel they made a mistake, but it is not fruitful to become angry, to call names, to "go ballistic." This creates interpersonal conflict, the type of conflict that is much more resistant to resolution than either task or administrative conflict.

The Positive Side of Conflict

Can there be anything positive about conflict? Yes, it is possible.

Conflict can Improve Decision Quality

It is often said that good ideas come from the crucible of debate. The concept of the dialectic has come to us from Plato and Socrates. The *dialectic* describes a three-step process of truth discovery. The steps are thesis, antithesis, and synthesis. Operationally Person A presents an assertion; this assertion is called the *thesis*. Next this assertion is countered by an assertion from Person B whose assertion notes the flaws in Person A's assertion; this is the *antithesis*. Person A and B argue and counter-argue in this way until their arguments are purged of flaws and a third assertion emerges, preserving and combining the best of A's and B's arguments. This third assertion is called the *synthesis*. Whether indeed it is the truth or the best decision possible, the synthesis emerges only after conflict, often heated, between the thesis and antithesis.

The dialectic survives today in a number of forms. First, in the courtroom, there is the plaintiff's lawyer, the accuser who asserts that the person on trial is guilty; this is the thesis. Next comes the defendant's lawyer who says the accused is innocent; this is the antithesis. During the trial the lawyers for the plaintiff and the defense argue and counter-argue. Hopefully, from this conflict the truth emerges in the minds of the jury whose verdict of guilty or innocent, as a result, is correct. The dialectic is also used in debate where debaters take the pro (thesis) and con (antithesis) sides and argue and counter-argue in the hope, theoretically at least, of finding truth. Finally, the dialectic is used in the Socratic teaching method. Here the teacher (on the antithesis side) counters and questions the students' assertions (on the thesis side). And as a result of this struggle between thesis and antithesis the truth will emerge; the student has learned.

Sometimes in groups and teams debate emerges spontaneously and can be very fruitful providing it does not provoke an interpersonal conflict simultaneously. Using debate in a group as part of a plan can be very productive. Suppose a tentative decision is made to implement a certain policy. A good way to test the temper of this decision is to divide a group into three subgroups; thesis, antithesis, and synthesis. The thesis (pro) and antithesis (con) groups debate and the synthesis group takes the best of both sides to incorporate into the proposed final decision.

Conflict Arouses

Conflict can emotionally *arouse* people; it can, therefore, move them from emotional zero. When people are aroused they are in a state of readiness. They are involved. The energy is there. If the conflict is inter-group, one group against another, it can be extremely motivating. It becomes an intense "us against them." When the conflict is intra-group (within a group), the situation is more difficult. Nonetheless, at times the arousal and the energy generated from it can be harnessed. For example, if two group members are arguing, you might suggest that indeed there might be value here. Suggest that the conflict be exploited and framed in the debate format. In doing this, a bitter argument might be transformed into a sanctioned argumentative form, the debate.

Conflict and Cohesion

In intense conflicts people become angry and, as a result, they often abandon their standards of good social behavior and their inhibitions. There is screaming, shouting, and name calling; the truth comes out. This is a critical point in a group and it can mark the point at which a group disintegrates. On the other hand, sometimes the group can begin to pick up the pieces and continue. When this happens the group is often more cohesive and bonded. Why? The members say, "If we made it through this, we can make it through anything." The feeling is somewhat similar to a family that survives a crisis.

Structured Conflict

At times group leaders will deliberately introduce conflict into a group with or without the group's knowledge. This is called *structured conflict*. There are a variety of ways to do this. The leader can, for example, give vital information, perks, or other valuables to some members and not others, and the non-rewarded members are made aware of the situation. This differential dispensing of rewards usually creates conflict. Another method is to introduce a "plant" into the group, a person who looks and acts like a regular member but is not. The "plant" has a hidden agenda. Sometimes it is to threaten; at other times it is to stir up intra-group conflict; and, occasionally, the "plant" acts as a spy.

Structured conflict is usually introduced into a group to create a "survival of the fittest" atmosphere. This is often the case in some work situations. Workers are threatened: "Produce or you're history." It is used to have some employees "beat up on" others in a "winner take all" contest. Or, it is used to report on employees to see which ones are troublemakers and should be dismissed or creatively discouraged in their present positions. Structured conflict can backfire in that group members can rebel against its use. It is a technique used infrequently where employees are skilled, valued, and in demand.

Summary

Stage 2, Storming, in Tuckman's group developmental sequence is characterized by conflict. This can prevent the group from becoming a group and interferes with task performance. The types of conflict that emerge in groups and teams can be personal, interpersonal, task, and administrative. Conflict can be managed using group or personal strategies. Finally, there can be some positive value to conflict.

CHAPTER 10

NORMING

In Tuckman's third stage of group development, *Norming*, conflicts are resolved, cohesiveness, compatibility, and conformity develop, new standards and roles emerge, and members can communicate more freely. In short, the group becomes a group and the "I's" become "We." The purpose of this chapter is to discuss the Norming process.

Cohesiveness

One key factor in bringing about the norming process is the emergence of cohesiveness. *Cohesiveness* can be defined as the glue that holds the group together. This is a metaphorical definition to be sure, but there is no acceptable objective definition of the term. Cohesiveness often follows a shared emotional experience. Soldiers who have fought together in war often form a bond that lasts a lifetime, meeting annually at reunions, sharing laughter and tears. Similar bonds are formed among athletes who have shared the fruits of victory, among patients who have suffered the same illness, among parents who have lost a child, and even among enemies who have fought against each other for long periods of time, for example. In groups and teams the shared emotional experience can result from conflict in the storming phase. If the conflict does not tear the group apart, it can generate a kind of cohesiveness manifested in the phrase, "If we made it through this, we can make it through anything."

Of course it is not a requirement that cohesiveness emerge from some dramatic emotional experience. Cohesiveness can emerge over time. For example, over time a group of skilled people can become cohesive as they progressively respect more and more the skills of their colleagues.

Researchers have noted that cohesive groups exhibit a number of characteristics in comparison with non-cohesive groups. Cohesive group members interact more, have interactions that are more positive, experience greater satisfaction from participating in the group, are influenced by other members more, influence other members more, are more productive, and are more effective in achieving goals.

Conformity

Norming can also be facilitated through the process of conforming. Group members conform when they think, perceive, and behave alike, and when they all begin to obey the same set of rules. A number of reasons for group conformity have been proposed.

Festinger's Group Locomotion Hypothesis

Festinger (1950) noted that groups have goals and must proceed in ways designed to allow them to achieve those goals. Goals are very important and a group's survival may depend on achieving a goal. For example, if a sales group is told that it must increase its sales ten percent per quarter, its survival (in this case survival means not being fired) is without question dependent upon reaching the goal. At some level of awareness, therefore, most groups assume that to reach (locomote toward) a goal, the members must conform. Pressure is put on those who do not. There is simply no time for tolerating individual idiosyncrasies.

Festinger's Social Comparison Theory

Festinger (1954) proposed a second reason for conforming in groups. Festinger noted that we tend to affiliate with those whose views are similar to ours and, as a result, a shared worldview is created. Because others in the group share our views, we feel that our ideas are agreed upon and confirmed. If one member does not share the predominant shared worldview, that member is judged to be deviant. And there is great pressure to conform. The social comparison mechanism works best in groups in which members are volunteers, not necessarily in the sense of working without pay, but, rather, because they voluntarily joined the group, which had extended invitations for membership.

Newcombe's ABX Theory

Underlying Newcombe's (1953, 1961) reason for group members' conforming is a very basic assumption: We like to be liked. And since we put a premium on being liked, we are willing to conform to a group's or another person's beliefs and attitudes if that conformation will initiate and maintain the state of being liked. Newcombe's theory seeks to explain how the process of being liked occurs. He assumes that we do not directly go up to people and say, "Would you like me? Would you be my friend?" This is a tactic that might be appropriate for a three- or four-year-old, but would be seen as rather pathetic and sad if an adult used it. Instead, the development and maintenance of the liking state is indirect and, according to Newcombe, it proceeds as follows: Let us suppose that Person A, an adult, wants Person B to like her. We have established that Person A will not ask Person B, "Would you please like me? Would you please be my friend?" What Person A must do instead is to determine the things that Person B likes and dislikes. Newcombe substituted Xs for things, and talked about a person's positive and negative orientations to Xs. Xs can be beliefs, attitudes, ideas, material things, or behavior.

If Person A is to get Person B to like her, she must first find Person B's orientation to as many Xs as possible. For example, she might learn that Person B believes that hard work will always be rewarded; that B harbors negative feelings toward cigarette smokers and sushi bars; that B loves to listen to new ideas; that B enjoys fine food, quality automobiles, and elegant clothes, and that B loves tennis, jogging, and hikes in the country. With this initial inventory of B's orientations to a number of Xs, Person A can begin to show positive orientations toward hard work, new ideas, fine food, quality automobiles, and elegant clothes, tennis, jogging, and hiking, while showing negative orientations toward smokers and sushi bars. Newcombe would predict that as Person A begins to take the same orientations as Person B toward a myriad of Xs Person B will begin to have a favorable reaction to or begin to like Person A. If this process continues and Person B indeed begins to like Person A, then Person A has achieved B's liking of her by conforming to B's orientations.

In groups, therefore, members continually conform by adopting the same orientations that other members have to a variety of Xs. They do this because they want to be liked.

Sherif, Sherif, and Nebergall's Social Judgment Theory

According to Sherif et al. (1965) people conform in a group, in many cases, because it is so easy to do so. Why? Because so many issues discussed in a group are not that important to one or more members. As a member of a group you may simply have no strong opinion about the refreshments for the next meeting or whether or not the meeting should begin at eight or nine o'clock. In addition, with more serious issues, you may be able to agree to any one of a number of possible decisions and, therefore, can conform with other members' preferences. Now and then an issue will arise about which you have strong feelings. In these situations you might not conform and, instead, decide to take up the fight. You will become ego involved, that is, become physically aroused: heightened pulse and respiration rates, and increased blood pressure. These physical responses show that you care, but, again, in a group the times at which you are so concerned about having your own point of view prevail are few; on other occasions you conform. Here there is no damage to your ego if you do conform.

Thibaut and Kelly's Social Exchange Theory

A final reason for conformity in groups is given by Thibaut and Kelly (1959) who take a marketplace view of group interactions. Thibaut and Kelly believe that we are motivated by our desire to gain *rewards* and avoid *costs*. Rewards and costs can be material or nonmaterial; in group interaction, however, they are mostly nonmaterial. Examples of rewards would be, "That's a great idea" or "We would like you to chair the committee." Included in the cost category would be statements from fellow group members that disagree with or question the merits of your suggestions. And one of the most devastating costs is to be isolated by the group, most often characterized by the withholding of eye contact and silence in response to your contributions.

In general, when an individual's rewards exceed costs, or in the market place metaphor, when income exceeds expenses, the tendency is to conform. In fact, the act of conforming is often the act that triggers the offering of rewards.

In some cases, however, even though rewards may exceed costs, conformity is not triggered. Why? Because the recipient of the rewards may withhold conformity in the hope of receiving even more rewards; perhaps income will be increased if conformity is not forthcoming. Of course, it is possible to push too far. The group may eventually view this behavior as disruptive and attempt to isolate or eject the offender.

Thibaut and Kelly note that pushing for more rewards may be related to the consequences of pushing. If you, as a group member, have other groups from which you might receive rich rewards, you might continue to push and risk rejection. For example, if you have three job offers on the table you may be more reckless than the employee who has no offers. The consequences of rejection would be minimal since you can go elsewhere for rewards. If other groups from which to gain rewards are not available, you will tend to be much more conservative, push less, and conform more.

If costs continually exceed rewards, you would most likely want to leave the group. There are a number of considerations here. Some groups are difficult to leave. You can physically separate yourself from your family but psychological separation is virtually impossible. In employment situations you can resign. This will reduce the costs incurred at work but may expose you to even greater costs, not only monetary, but costs to your self-concept as well. If you remain unemployed you will have no answer to the question, "What do you do?"

Groupthink

In general, group cohesiveness and conformity are desirable states to which a group should ordinarily aspire. Janis (1982), however, has noted that sometimes groups become so cohesive and conforming that group morale and uniformity of opinion become more important than the critical analysis of ideas. Janis called this Groupthink. He noted that groupthink groups:

- *Feel Invincible*: "We are invincible. Nobody can touch us."
- *Have Illusions of Morality*: "What we are doing is the right thing."
- *Have Collective Rationalization*: "We can explain and justify our actions."
- *Have Shared Stereotypes*: "We are the good. They are the bad." Often the "bad" are those who disagree with the groupthink group.
- *Have Self-Censorship*: The groupthink group keeps secrets.
- *Have Illusions of Consensus*: The group appears to unanimously agree on all matters.
- *There is Great Pressure to Conform*: Group members fear the consequences that might occur if they deviate from the "party line."
- *Self-Appointed Mind Guards Emerge*: These mind guards serve to protect the group against information critical or damaging to the group. A present-day mind guard is the "spin doctor," a person who twists or spins negative information into positive information. For example, a politician may vote against a bill that would increase funds for environmental protection. The politician learns that his constituents were really for the bill. How can the politician spin a story about his vote? He calls a news conference for the next day and announces that he voted against the bill because it was not strong enough, that he is really for environmental protection, and that he will vote for it as soon as a stronger bill is drafted.

In the United States groupthink is said to have been responsible for a number of failures in foreign policy: the Bay of Pigs invasion during the Kennedy administration, the Vietnam War during the Johnson administration, Watergate during the Nixon administration, and Irangate during the Reagan administration, for instance. In each case a small group of strategists planned and executed policies and insulated themselves from outside suggestions and criticisms. And, the groupthink effect was magnified in those situations because the respective groups were able to work under the cover of the top secret designation.

Groupthink effects are most marked in groups whose activities affect others. The groups can be major governmental policy groups or, by comparison, minor groups, religious organization boards, school boards, boards for service clubs, and so on. Groups whose activities do not affect others may be groupthink groups but without consequence. Notable here would be social groups whose goals are to have fun and enjoy the companionship of others.

Combating Groupthink

A number of suggestions have been offered to combat groupthink. Among them are:

- *Encourage Independent Critical Thinking*: Here the goal is to have each member take a separate view of a problem and make a solitary analysis if it.

- *Assign a Devil's Advocate*: When someone becomes a candidate for sainthood in the Roman Catholic Church, a devil's advocate is appointed. This person is to represent the devil and is to find all the negative information about the candidate that would argue against sainthood status. Applying this concept to a groupthink group, the group should assign the devil's advocate role to a member and in this role the member should criticize every proposed action of the group.

- *Suggest Alternative Decision-Making Strategies*: For every policy that is suggested, an alternative policy should also be suggested and pro and con arguments should be made for each.

- *Invite Outsiders to Review a Group's Work*: An independent outsider can often view things in a new and fresh way. The outsider should have no vested interest in any of the group's ideas and should be able to see if the group is going down a blind alley.
- *Make the Group's Information Public*: All of us behave differently in public than we do in private and so it is with groups. Secrecy is a key ingredient in the groupthink process. When the veil of secrecy is removed, the group's activities become open to criticism and change.

Groupthink Phenomenon Questioned

Not all writers support Janis' belief about the pervasive existence of groupthink. Bower (1995a, p. 329), for example, reported that a review of 496 group decision studies published between 1985 and 1994 showed that, contrary to groupthink theory, the best decisions occur in *tight-knit* groups addressing tough problems. Moreover, Bower notes that experimental groups working cooperatively outperform most individuals in those groups on problem-solving tasks, and they usually do about as well as the sharpest solo decision maker in a group.

Compatibility

> Jack Sprat would eat no fat,
> His wife would eat no lean.
> Together when they supped,
> They licked the platter clean

Compatibility refers to a state in which people's predispositions, skills, and behaviors are *symmetrical* or *complementary*. The *symmetrical* state is one of sameness. We tend to get along with those who have the same predispositions and skills as we have and who behave as we do.

In addition, we tend to get along with people whose predispositions, skills, and behaviors go together and reinforce one another so that the whole is indeed greater than the sum of its parts. If one group member has great task skills and another great interpersonal support and facilitation skills, the two individuals *complement* each other; each offers the group something the other does not. In Chapter 1 it was noted that a defining characteristic of teams is that members have complementary skills. Starting a business, for example, requires an accountant, an attorney, and a manager. Each brings something to the table that the others do not.

An advantage that a compatible group has, especially if it is complementary, is that there are few conflicts. Members do not compete with one another claiming that they know more than a fellow group member. Each member has an area of expertise and, therefore, knowledge of that area that other members do not have. Often complementary relationships have been compared to the biological concept of symbiosis where two organisms co-exist by feeding off one another. A small bird survives by pecking food from the teeth of a rhinoceros, which in turn survives longer as a result of this dental hygiene.

Of all task groups, a compatible group probably "becomes a group" or norms sooner than other groups. From the outset the role of each member is known, accountant, attorney, clergy, computer programmer, engineer, and so on. The roles have a long history of acceptance. Therefore, little time and struggle is spent on role definition.

In many groups compatibility creation is not possible because there is no control of member selection. This is certainly true for volunteer groups and for non-volunteer groups where, for example, everyone from a certain division, department, or area is required to attend meetings. Here it may take longer for the group to "become a group" and repeat visits back to the storming stage may occur.

Summary

In this chapter we have discussed *Norming*. It is the stage of group development where the group becomes a group. Power struggles are resolved, interpersonal squabbles are resolved, and administrative procedures are agreed upon. In general the conflicts are over. During the norming process groups become cohesive and group members conform to the standards of the group. It is possible that cohesiveness and conformity can lead to a situation called groupthink, a process that warps reasoning and moral judgment, especially on complex matters. On the other hand, there is the position that groupthink effects are not as widespread as reported. Finally, the process of norming seems to be facilitated if group members are compatible.

CHAPTER 11

PERFORMING: PART ONE
PROBLEM SOLVING

At some point the successful group settles down and begins to do what it is supposed to do: complete its task. At this juncture conflicts have been resolved or managed, the group has become cohesive, and members have begun to conform. When this stage is reached it is time for the group to perform. Performance of a task group consists mainly of problem solving and presenting the results of the problem-solving deliberations to a target audience. In this chapter we will discuss problem-solving and idea-generation techniques, and, in the next chapter, group presentations will be discussed.

Problem Solving

Definition

A *problem* is a situation that causes physical or psychological discomfort to some party. Problems can range from the very simple and inconsequential, the new puppy is not yet housetrained, for example, to the complex and grave, matters of life and death and war and peace, for instance. While we often speak of problems in very general terms, the drug problem, the energy problem, the education problem, and so on, it is best for group operations to verbally express every problem by beginning the expression with a question word: Who? What? When? Where? Why? and How? This operationalizes the problem and brings it into focus for the deliberative group or team. Consider the following pairs:

- "The Drug Problem" vs "How can we teach children about the harmful effects of drugs?"
- "The Education Problem" vs "What can we do to get elementary school children interested in mathematics and science?"

In each of the above pairs the latter member of the pair is much more specific and gives direction to the group or team that is charged with solving the problem.

Types of Problems

Problems of Fact

The *problem of fact* revolves around a question whose answer or solution is available or determinable. Problems of fact are the most easily solved problems. How high is the Sears Tower in Chicago or the CN Tower in Toronto? Answers can be easily obtained from a number of sources.

Problems of fact require virtually no deliberation but just research, often minimal research. When people deliberate or discuss problems of fact at any length, it is usually symptomatic of another need. People may just want to talk and argue. Patrons at a sports bar may argue endlessly about who hit the most home runs back when. This question can be solved in minutes in myriad ways. But to solve it ends the interaction, and it is the interaction that is desired, not the solution.

Problems of Belief, Value, and Attitude

Problems of belief, value, and attitude revolve around the most cherished ideas that people can hold. They are, therefore, the most difficult problems to solve. One problem of belief, attitude, and value is the problem of abortion. In 1973 the United States Supreme Court ruled in Roe v. Wade that states may not ban abortion in the first six months of a pregnancy, that a fetus is not a "person" protected by the 14th amendment to the U.S. Constitution, and the amendment protects a woman from state intrusion into her decision to bear or not to bear a child. Since that decision the battle lines have been drawn. The problem in the battle, of course, is, "When does life begin?" Does it begin at conception, at birth, or at some point between conception and birth? No group or team constituted of members on opposing sides of the issue since 1973 has been able to solve this problem.

Some of our most cherished beliefs, values, and attitudes concern religion and, therefore, it is not surprising that many problems of beliefs, values, and attitudes are anchored to religion. The abortion problem certainly is. Territorial disputes in Northern Ireland and Jerusalem are as well. Ranking second to religion as a cause of belief, value, and attitude problems is culture, from cultures as large as countries to the subcultures within countries to the individual family. A problem for families is, "How can we maintain our family values in an electronic media-saturated environment?" On a larger scale, Native Americans ask, "How can we preserve our culture and our language in the society that has been forced upon us?" And at the country level, one might ask, "How can we preserve our national identity and values in a world dominated by global media?"

If problems were arranged on a scale that ran from easily solvable to unsolvable, problems of belief, values, and attitude would cluster most closely around the unsolvable.

Forensic Problems

A forensic problem is one of discovery when the group or team through its deliberations attempts to discover something about the past. Included would be the problems:

- Who did it?
- When did it happen?
- Why did it happen?
- Where did it happen?
- How did it happen?

Forensic problems are the problems discussed in courtrooms where some past event is discussed for the purpose of declaring one party innocent and the other guilty. Forensic problems are the target, too, of forensic medicine where the forensic physician is called in on homicide cases to answer the "Why" and "How" questions bulleted above. Forensic anthropologists enter the scene as well, often focusing their skills on skeletons centuries old or contemporary finds where only skeletons, teeth, and jewelry may remain. Indeed, the task of the historian is forensic in nature. Trying to know, understand, and interpret the past is a most difficult problem.

Problems of Policy

A *problem of policy* deals with the future and focuses on the procedures and guidelines that are to be devised for and deployed in the future. Most prominent in deliberating problems of policy are legislators who discuss and debate (1) the rules (laws) by which we must live in the future, and (2) the present laws that need to be modified or changed. Of course policy problems are not confined to legislative bodies. Almost any group will discuss problems of policy. A local service club may discuss "How can we raise money?" and then follow this with a discussion of the problem, "To whom should this money raised be donated?"

Problems of policy have a positive aspect because they deal with the future and the future holds the possibility that things can get better or be improved. The past can be regretted or cherished but it cannot be changed. The alcoholic member of AA can tell family members and friends, "I'm sorry for all the terrible things I've done," but he cannot change those things. He can only plan for a better future. In like manner, citizens may be disenchanted with the past performance of their legislators, but the legislators can always promise that the future will be better.

Problem Sources

Inherited Problems

Inherited problems are problems passed on to a group or team by other groups or teams. There are no surprises. The recipient group knows in advance about the impending transmission. At a personal level, if you plan to marry and you know that your intended spouse has $27,000 in credit card debt, you have an inherited problem if you follow through with the wedding. At a group level, if you are a member of a nominating committee charged with picking candidates to run for office in a group to which you belong, and you know that the last nominating committee was charged with bias and favoritism, then you have inherited an image problem.

Assigned Problems

Assigned problems are the most common problems. You are a member or are assigned to a group, and your group is assigned a problem. On a construction job it might be "How can we protect bridge workers from the hot exhaust from trains running beneath the bridge?" For a group in a profit or non-profit organization it might be "How can we reduce costs five percent in each of the next four quarters?" For the community soccer league a group could be assigned the problem, "What can be done to have all children participate and still have a competitive league?"

Discovered Problems

Discovered problems are the surprise problems and the surprises are often not happy surprises. If you do get married and find out after the wedding that your new spouse has $27,000 in credit card debt, then you have a discovered problem. If your community soccer group buys a field for practice and play and discovers after the sale that the ground is saturated with toxic materials, then your group has a discovered problem.

Framing the Problem

Before deliberations begin on a problem the problem should be put into question format and the overall goal (not necessarily the solution) should be stated. As mentioned above, stating the problem in question format using one of the "Why?" or "How?" words, provides focus, specificity, and direction. In like manner, those same gains accrue when the overall goal is stated. For example, if the community soccer league's goal is to have every child on the team play and still have a competitive league, the league's deliberative group is given focus, specificity, and direction in the charge. At the same time, the goal does not dictate the final solution.

The Problem Solving Process

The problem solving process includes gathering information on the problem, reasoning with that information, generating new ideas to solve the problem, analyzing the audience, deciding upon a solution, and implementing the solution. We shall use the community soccer league as our example as we discuss these steps.

Information Gathering

The first step in the problem solving process is to gather information about the problem. This requires research. The research effort today has been immensely enhanced by the Internet. The community soccer league group assigned the problem, "How can we have every child play in every game and still maintain a competitive league?" might search for information on similar leagues throughout the country. They might also talk to other community groups and ask them what procedures they follow with regard to the problem. There are few problems that only one group faces. Therefore, it is a good assumption that other communities are facing and discussing the same problem.

Reasoning with the Gathered Information

Information is virtually useless unless action is taken to cognitively process it. This action is called *reasoning.* Three common types of reasoning are *deductive, inductive,* and *analogic.*

Deductive Reasoning

In *deductive reasoning* we reason from a broad generalization to a specific conclusion. Consider this syllogism:

- *Major Premise:* People who take a course in small group and team communication perform better in groups than people who do not.

- *Minor Premise:* Mary took a course in small group and team communication.
- *Conclusion:* Mary will perform better in groups than people who have not taken a course.

How can the soccer group use deductive reasoning? For example, in their research they might have found a soccer league that solved the problem that they are trying to solve. We'll call the league "Perfect League." Then our soccer group can begin its reasoning with the major premise, if any soccer league does what Perfect League does then that league will be able to play all children and still have a competitive league. If our soccer group adopts this major premise and indeed does everything that Perfect League does, then our soccer group's problem will be solved.

Inductive Reasoning

In *inductive reasoning* you reason from a set of specific instances to a general conclusion. If you worked with 100 groups over a period of three years you might have discovered that in groups where people took a course in small group and team communication, group performance was better than in those groups where a course was not taken. You would be using your information from 100 specific instances to arrive at a general conclusion. This is inductive reasoning. Our soccer group might gather information on 20 other soccer leagues and find specific instances in each league where the investigated leagues had success in playing all children while remaining competitive. From these 20 instances, our soccer group might come to a general conclusion, an induction, about how it might solve its problem

Reasoning by Analogy

When you reason by analogy you find a second situation with similarities to the one with which you are dealing and then try to determine if the dynamics in the second situation can be used to think about the one with which you are dealing. Advances in medicine were aided by analogic reasoning. The heart and the circulatory system were not fully understood until the water pump was invented; similarly, the nervous system had not begun to be understood until electricity was generated and electrical transmission systems were developed. Physicians analogize from pumps and electrical systems to understand the human body.

Our soccer group too can reason by analogy. For example, the group might say, "Let's compare our children's soccer league to the National Football League's exhibition season, i.e., the pre-season games that do not affect a team's final standing. The NFL has the task of making pre-season games interesting (meaning competitive) while at the same time playing all the players; this is the time when all players, particularly the rookies, must be evaluated. Therefore, in a sense, the NFL is doing what we want to do in our soccer league. We can then reason by analogy from the NFL to our soccer league.

Generating New Ideas

Often in attempting to solve a problem the information gathered is insufficient to enable a group or team to come to a solution. More ideas must be generated. In this section we will discuss a number of idea generation techniques. Included are role playing, metaphorical thinking, fantasy chaining, brainstorming, buzz groups, the nominal groups technique, the Delphi technique, focus groups, projective techniques, and chat rooms. Most of these techniques can be conducted face-to-face or in a computer-mediated mode.

Role Playing

In *role playing* an attempt is made to gain new perceptions and ideas about a problem by having group members participate in a drama. A scenario and a plot are created. Characters in the drama are identified and their roles are defined. Then the drama is enacted; players must try to "walk in the shoes" of their characters. Role playing is used extensively in sales training. One plays the seller, another the potential buyer. In our soccer group, the group might try having parents with skillful soccer-playing children role play parents with poor and mediocre soccer-playing children and vice versa.

Metaphorical Thinking

The metaphorical thinking technique is similar to reasoning by analogy. A metaphor is a word or idea that stands in place of another word or idea suggesting a likeness between the two. If we say "John is a lion," we are using a metaphor and are suggesting that the attributes of a lion can be used to describe John. The Austrian market researcher, Hans Dichter, was famous for using metaphors to design products. For example, he had blindfolded test subjects hold and hug an array of computer keyboards, telling the subjects that the keyboards were their lovers, their pets, and so on. He would then ask the subjects to describe the keyboards in response to the metaphor. Our soccer group might be asked to use the family metaphor, that each team is a family, and if it were your family, how would you treat your "children"?

Fantasy Chaining

Sometimes in a group, particularly when the group is tired and weary, members start to become giddy and silly. This is usually viewed in a negative light. However, it can be the launching point for creative activity. *Fantasy chaining* occurs when members depart from reality and take a fantasy trip. Members may imagine that they are flying, that they can see through walls, that they have just uncorked the genie from the bottle, and so on. When others members join in, the chaining occurs. Children are very good at this because they are not ashamed to play make believe.

Brainstorming

Brainstorming refers to a specific set of procedures for generating ideas. The basic assumption of brainstorming is that *quantity produces quality.* If you produce enough ideas you will produce the best ideas. Unfortunately the term, brainstorming, has taken on a generic meaning used for any situation in which people throw out a few ideas. But, as created by Osborne (1993, 1953), the technique has specific rules and steps.

The Rules for Brainstorming

- Adverse Criticism is Taboo: There can be no criticism, verbal or nonverbal. Criticism inhibits the generation of ideas.
- Freewheeling is welcome: Brainstorming participants must just "let go."
- Quantity of ideas is desired: Remember quantity produces quality.
- The combination and improvement of ideas is welcome: One member's idea can trigger a thought in another member who builds on the initial idea.

Following the brainstorming session a second group takes the ideas generated by the brainstorming group and does the following:
- Categorizes the generated ideas.
- Critically evaluates the ideas.
- Generates new ideas.
- Makes final recommendations with reference to the problem for which the brainstorming occurred.

The second group is brought in because of the tendency of people to not like to criticize their own ideas or to hear others criticize their ideas. A fresh second group is used; this group is assumed to have no vested interest in any of the ideas.

The Buzz Group or Phillips 66 Technique

In the *buzz group or Phillips 66 technique* a large group is divided into small groups of six, then each six-member group is asked to deliberate on the problem at hand for six minutes, and at the end of six minutes one member of each group reports its findings to the larger group. The technique was developed by J.D. Phillips of Phillips Petroleum. Phillips found that when a large group is blocked on a problem, the block can be removed and a solution or progress to a solution can be made by following the steps that were just recited.

The Nominal Group and Delphi Techniques

The *Nominal Group Technique* and the *Delphi Technique* are both ideal when group members are geographically separated, and when there is a dominant or disruptive member in a group. In the latter situation it is sometimes best to treat group members as though they were physically separated, and run the Nominal Group and Delphi Techniques over a computer network with participants working alone with their computers. This can be done with a Listserve facility or various email configurations. The configuration should be asynchronous, that is, one message should follow another and there can be no interruptions. The steps in the respective techniques follow:

The Nominal Group Technique (NGT)

1. Identify the Problem
2. Group members independently write their solutions on cards
3. The solutions are collected, read, and then placed in public view.

4. The solutions are then discussed.

5. Next have individuals privately rank each solution on a ten-point scale. Sum the ranking for each idea.

6. Report the rankings, from highest to lowest, and discuss.

7. Take a final vote on which solutions are to be implemented, or, if there is still widespread disagreement, a second ranking might be done and a second vote taken.

8. If the situation is one where only one solution can be implemented, then the vote should include only three or four of the solutions ranked highest.

The Delphi Technique

1. Identify the problem and prepare an open-ended questionnaire about the problem and send it to select individuals.

2. Analyze the responses and redraft a more specific questionnaire and send it to the same people.

3. Tally the responses from the second questionnaire narrowing down the options. Send out ballots, listing possible decisions, for multiple rankings. If the option list is long, this might be repeated. Repeat this step until a decision is made.

4. Follow up with a report to all participants.

The Focus Group Technique

A *focus group* is a temporary group created to produce insights about an issue or problem through the medium of group interaction. Paramount in this definition is the *group interaction medium*. It is assumed that group interaction will yield insights not released by the use of other methodologies, polls, surveys, and interviews, for example. People who conduct focus groups must be sensitive to the language of the focus group participants.

The words that the participants use provide insights into the way the participants think and feel.

In conducting a focus group each participant is told to think about (focus on) a particular problem and to prepare an *individual statement* on the problem, telling their experiences related to the problem. The individual statements are written. When the individual statements are completed, the focus group begins by having participants present their individual statements in turn without discussion.

Following this the focus group discussion begins. Participants discuss the problem and learn what common and different experiences they have had concerning the problem. From this discussion possible solutions to the problem may emerge or may be deduced from the discussion.

One master of using focus group methodology has been Dick Morris. Over a period of years, Morris was selected to solve these problems for President Clinton: "How can I get elected as governor, as president, and reelected as president?" Morris ran focus groups, almost non-stop, and extracted phrases from the participants' interactive language. These participants dealt with this problem: "What kind of person would you like your president to be?" The extracted phrases then became part of Clinton's speeches. One such phrase was "not a single child." Think of how many ways this can be used: "not a single child should go to bed hungry, not a single child should be deprived of a good education, not a single child should be without health insurance," and so on. Words and phrases that come from the people (in focus groups) resonate with the people and can be used to persuade them in turn.

Projective Techniques

Another set of techniques that can generally be used to address the problem of how people think or feel are the *projective techniques*. In using the projective techniques you present essentially meaningless stimuli to participants in order to see what meaning they *project* onto these stimuli.

Suppose you are on a citizens' committee charged to assess the image that your town presents to visitors. The problem would be, "How is our town perceived by visitors?" To approach this problem using the projective techniques you might have visitors respond to questions such as these:

- If our town were an animal, what animal would it be?
- If our town were an automobile, what make of automobile would it be?
- If our town were a color, what color would it be?

The questions may seem silly but the answers participants give can yield insights into the problem. For example, if your town were said to be a race horse, a Maserati, and the color, red, what meanings would the participants be projecting? Included would be the qualities of sleekness, streamlined, power, speed, warmth, and friendliness, the qualities associated with racehorses, Jaguars, and the color red.

Chat Rooms

Recently computer chat rooms have begun to be used to solve problems. The chat rooms are cheaper and faster than focus groups and surveys. Keenan (2001) presented examples of the use of this technique in business. Hallmark hosts an online chat room for 200 consumers who chat about everything from holiday decorating ideas to prayers for the sick. From monitoring these chats, Hallmark gets a lot of ideas for cards. Coca-Cola created a chat room for teenagers to get ideas on how to remake its Powerade drink. Kraft Foods chatted with 160 individuals about frozen vegetables.

Conducting focus groups in the traditional way is very labor intensive. The verbal interactions must be transcribed. With chat rooms, on the other hand, no transcription is necessary since participants type in their messages. These messages are, therefore, computer ready and can be printed immediately, or computer analyzed to identify key words and phrases or to compute the frequency of occurrence of certain words, and so on.

Audience Analysis

Problems are solved for someone or some party or for a group or an audience of some kind. Remember our definition of problem: A situation that causes physical or psychological discomfort to some party. The aggrieved party is the audience for problem solvers. If the problem-solving group's solution does not please the audience, the audience remains aggrieved. It behooves the problem-solving group, therefore, to analyze the audience whom they serve. Three types of audience analysis are demographic, attitudinal, and goal determination.

A *demographic* analysis determines the age, gender, income, status, political registry, religion, and so on, of audience members. To get an idea of audience analysis you might want to log in to the U.S. Census website at census.gov. Plug in your zip code and see a brief demographic analysis of the area in which you live.

An *attitudinal* audience analysis assesses how an audience feels about a number of issues. "Does life begin at conception?" "Should the drinking age be lowered to 18 years?" and "Should doctor-assisted suicide be legalized?" are examples of attitudinal inquiries.

A *goal determination* audience analysis attempts to determine just what solution would solve the audience's problem. This is not always easy since different audience members have different expectations.

In situations that we label as political (not limited to government bodies), audience analysis becomes complex. Suppose the local soccer boosters buy land to make a soccer field. On the surface a simple task: just plant the turf, install the goals, chalk-line the boundaries, and erect some seating. But soon the boosters find that there will be a zoning hearing (the neighbors are upset), that the unions are upset because a non-union contractor has been hired to do the civil engineering work, and the EPA is upset because a small patch of wetlands will be sacrificed. Therefore, what began as a solution to a simple problem, "Where can our children play soccer?" with an audience limited to families of children who play soccer, now includes a multiple audience, each having a separate vested interest.

Deciding Upon A Solution

Problem-solving groups, through information gathering, reasoning, and idea generation, eventually produce one or more potential solutions for the problem at hand. An audience analysis helps show the best match between one or more of the possible solutions and the needs and expectations of the audience.

Before making a final recommendation, the problem-solving group should check to see if there are resources available to implement its proposed solution. Resources include physical resources, qualified personnel, money, and time. A solution may be a good one but, if there is no talent, money, or time available to implement the solution, it is no solution. When resources are limited, and they usually are, a tactic that is often used in evaluating solutions is the *mini-max* tactic. Here what problem-solving groups do is to evaluate each proposed solution on (1) how much the solution would cost in terms of resources if implemented and (2) the extent to which each proposed solution would solve the problem. Then the proposed solutions are rank ordered in terms of maximum effect on solving the problem and minimum resource cost.

Summary

Solving problems is the key function of task groups. This chapter has reviewed the problem-solving process. "Problem" was defined, the types of problems were discussed, problem sources were revealed, steps in the problem-solving process were presented, a battery of idea-generation techniques was detailed, audience analysis was referenced, and solution selection was examined.

CHAPTER 12

PERFORMING: PART TWO

GROUP PRESENTATIONS

In this chapter we will discuss the basic principles of group presentations and then identify and discuss a number of types of presentation formats.

Group Presentation Principles

Acro means tip or top and *nym* means name so an *acronym* is a word made from the tips or tops or first letters of other words. In discussing the basic principles of group presentations there are two important acronyms to consider: **COP** and **RAMP**.

COP

Content

The "C" in COP refers to content. No presentation can be given unless there is content to deliver. Typically in group presentations the content delivered will be a mix of the group's information-gathering activities and the results of the group's deliberations. To use a construction metaphor, content consists of all the basic materials you need to begin.

Organization

The "O" in COP refers to organization. The best content in the world cannot inform and persuade unless it is organized in some way. All the building materials delivered to a construction site are worthless unless organized in the structure of a building. A number of common schemes for organizing content are recognized.

- *Chronological*: In chronological organization content is organized from past to present to future or vice versa. An excellent example of chronological organization is Lincoln's Gettysburg Address. Lincoln began with a reference to the past: "Four score and seven years ago...." He then moved to the present: "Now we are engaged in a great civil war...." He then addressed the future: "It is for us the living, rather, to be dedicated to the unfinished work...." The short speech is a masterpiece.

- *Spatial*: In spatial organization content is presented by referring to various locations. Viewers of the weather channel see fine use of spatial organization. Weather on the east coast, the Gulf region, the interior Mississippi valley, the Plains, the Rockies, and the west coast regions is reported. A problem-solving group trying to assess the problems caused by a new limited-access highway might also refer to geographical regions: the suburbanites who want the highway, the shop owners who live on the present access road who do not want the highway, and so on.

- *Topical*: In topical organization content is organized around topic clusters. For example, if a problem-solving civic group is reporting on the local public schools, the group might organize its presentation on the topics of teaching, facilities, support services, and so on.

- *Analogy*: Analogical organization requires the use of metaphor, thus introducing a second word, idea, thing, or process and applying the attributes of the second to the issue at hand. A problem-solving group charged with providing solutions for maintaining a run-down school building might use the sports conditioning mantra, "No Pain, No Gain," for example. Here they might recommend a costly (pain) and complete renovation of the school to provide, once and for all, a sound, safe, and functional school. Just as individuals will never get in shape unless they are willing to suffer the pain, so too will the school in question never be sound, safe, and functional until the citizens suffer the pain.

- *Cause and Effect*: In cause-to-effect reasoning presenters examine a certain situation, past or present, and then report on or project the consequences of that situation. A public health awareness group might investigate the eating habits of young adults and then project from this investigation the effects that will result from the observed dietary habits.

- *Mixed Formats*: Of course a presentation can have a mix of organizational schemes. Certainly the cause-to-effect and effect-to-cause schemes imply chronology. And the reporter on the weather channel can talk about the location of a moving weather front yesterday, today, and tomorrow, thus mixing spatial and chronological formats.

Presentation

The "P" in COP refers to *presentation*. The best content expertly organized may have little or no effect on an audience unless it is presented well. And, sometimes poor content poorly organized has a persuasive effect on an audience because of the presentational dynamics. More reference to presentation will be made in the following paragraphs.

RAMP

Reason

The "R" in RAMP refers to the *reason* for the presentation. Why is the group giving a presentation? It would seem that this is so obvious that it does not even deserve mention. But obvious things are sometimes forgotten or blurred. Visitors to websites will often see, at the top of the site, a mission statement which reveals the reason for the existence of the organization behind the site. Group presentations often begin by stating the group's charge or the task assigned to them. Then the group states its reason for communicating: to report specifically on how it responded to the charge or task it was given.

Audience

The "A" in RAMP refers to the *audience*. Any presenting group must try to understand its audience. Some of the techniques for doing this, attitudinal and demographics surveys, for example, were discussed in the previous chapter. Another key process to be considered is *identification*. When you identify with an audience you show the audience that you are one of them.

You can try to identify with an audience by learning as much about the audience as possible. Then you can tell the audience members how you like where they live, how you like their sports teams, how people tell you how nice the people are here, how sympathetic you are with respect to their problems, and so on. Nonverbally, you can identify with people in the audience by dressing like them, by eating and liking their food, by driving vehicles like they do, and so on. You must not exaggerate in these efforts; if you do you will be seen as a phony.

Medium

The "M" in RAMP refers to medium. Common presentational media are face-to-face, written, and electronic. Each medium has certain requirements. In face-to-face situations, for example, presenters must repeat more because audience members cannot look back as they do with text, rewind, or click on the back button as they might do respectively with videotape or on the net.

Of course live presentations are often augmented with other media, microphones, overheads, slide projectors, LCD projectors, live internet connections, and so on. A good thing for the presenting group to remember is that these auxiliary media are to serve in a supporting role. The group must always remain the center of focus. Projections should not be a center of focus. Projections should be on screens on the group's periphery with the group remaining front and center and well lighted.

In the future, electronic media presentations will be transmitted more and more on the internet. Those planning to present on the internet will need to consider some aspects of that medium: the internet is global, collapsing space; the internet audience does not read so much as it scans; and the internet audience is impatient, abandoning sites within seconds, for example.

Presenters

The "P" in RAMP refers to the presenters themselves. Their characteristics and actions can enhance or lessen the effectiveness of a group presentation. Three important factors that can affect presenter effectiveness are *ethos*, *logos*, and *pathos*.

- *Ethos* refers to the credibility, trustworthiness, or believability of a presenter. Presenters can have absolute truth, but, if no one believes them, they will not be able to successfully communicate that truth. And those who have ethos can successfully communicate the truth and falsehood (at least until they are caught).

- *Logos* refers to the intellectual soundness of presentations. Do the presenters use credible information and evidence, is proper reasoning used in the processing of information and evidence, and are logical conclusions drawn?

- *Pathos* refers to the emotion generated in the audience by the presenters. To persuade an audience, the audience must be moved from emotional zero. The move can be in a positive direction toward joy, happiness, and enchantment, or in a negative direction toward fear, anxiety, and terror.

In thinking about ethos, logos, and pathos presenters should consider the audience. Some audiences are impressed or persuaded by logical (logos) appeals, while others respond more favorably to emotional (pathos) appeals. Credibility and believability (ethos) are almost always a positive presenter attribute. In some cases, presenters risk losing their ethos. For example, presenters who use emotional appeals before an audience that expects logical arguments can lose their ethos.

Group Presentation Formats

Certain group presentation formats have become traditional. Three prominent formats are the *panel*, the *forum*, and the *symposium*.

The Panel

In a *panel* a small group discusses a problem before an audience. The group members are selected on the basis of their having expertise on the problem and they discuss the problem amongst themselves. A moderator guides the discussion. The audience is essentially passive and does not interact actively with the presenters.

What the audience observes is a group of experts participating in the problem-solving process. There are no set speeches and there is no set order for group members to speak. If any interaction management is required, the moderator steps in.

Panel members should be elevated on a platform; they should be visible and audible to one another and the audience. Panels should be permitted to run for at least 90 minutes so all arguments can be presented and criticized, and so the group can come to a solution for the problem.

At the end of the panel session the moderator should summarize the session and obtain confirmation from the panel members that the summary fairly represented their views.

The Forum

In a *forum* an entire audience gets a chance to discuss a problem or topic. The forum is led by a chairperson who sets the rules for the audience's participation, triggers the beginning of the interaction by asking leading questions or making controversial statements, and thereafter manages the interaction. Audience members make impromptu speeches from the floor and then answer questions and criticisms about their statements. When it works well, the forum is an information-sharing process that can lead to problem solutions.

Observing the forum is a small group of individuals, one of whom is the chairperson of the forum. This small observational group is usually the group that arranged the forum. Small groups that arrange and conduct forums are usually fact-finding groups. They can be town councils, school boards, legislative subcommittees, boards of trustees for profit and non-profit groups, and so on.

At times the forum can become a shouting contest where volume and loudness rule. When this happens the forum process breaks down. Some steps can be taken to restore order, shutting off shouters' microphones, for instance, but it is a difficult situation to control. The best preventive measure is for the chairperson to establish the rules at the beginning of the session and enforce them.

At times the audience is victimized by the group that arranges and conducts the forum. Local government leaders may have decided upon a tax increase. Expecting a public outcry they schedule a forum or public hearing. Behind closed doors the hearing may be referred to, quite cynically, as a "twist and shout" session, or a "Let's go make fools of the dorks" session, and indeed the exercise is often quite cynical. The chairperson sets or enforces no rules and the forum turns into chaos duly recorded by the nighttime news crew whose edited film makes the citizens look like fools. Or, a second tactic is planting certain pro-tax-increase citizens in the audience so the fact finders can say, "Some want the increase and some do not." This sends a message to the larger public that the voters are split on the issue. So the forum, like any other technique, can be corrupted.

The Colloquium

The colloquium is a blend of the panel and the forum. In the colloquium a group of three to six expert participants discuss a problem among themselves and with an audience, and under the direction of a moderator. A colloquium is a public discussion where experts and lay people (the audience) interact to solve a problem.

The Symposium

A *symposium* consists of a small group of experts who deliver a series of speeches on a given problem before an audience. The purpose is to inform the audience about the problem. The symposium format is more formal than the colloquium, panel, or forum. The speeches are delivered uninterrupted by question or comment. The interaction in a symposium is managed by a chairperson who introduces the speakers, making sure speakers stay within the allotted time for their speeches. Preplanning is necessary, of course, to ensure that speakers do not duplicate other speakers' efforts and that all aspects of the problem are covered.

The symposium members should be seated on a platform and should be visible and audible to one another and the audience. Generally a symposium lasts about 90 minutes.

At the end of a symposium several things can be done. Often the symposium group will shift to panel mode and discuss the problem and related issues among themselves but before the audience. This can be followed by a Q and A (Question and Answer) session or even a forum if time permits. Whatever the follow-up format is, there should be enough time allocated to the follow-up session to make it meaningful.

Reviewing Public Presentation Formats

The public presentation formats just presented all depend upon qualified and dedicated participants. All formats must be managed by a chairperson or moderator. If not well managed the formats can all lead to chaos. Each format has its advantages and disadvantages. The symposium, the most formal, allows essentially no interaction among symposium members or with the audience. But it does allow each member to speak without interruption. The panel permits interaction among panel members, but this can lead to one panel member dominating the discussion. Again, there is virtually no communication with the audience. In the forum the audience rules since they are the speakers, the commentators, the questioners, and the critics. A colloquium is a blend of the panel and the forum.

In cases where time permits perhaps the best scenario for public group presentations would be to do the symposium first, the panel second, and the forum last. You would then begin by hearing, without interruption, experts speak on the problem, then discuss it among themselves, and finally listen to the audience speak on and discuss the problem.

Summary

Group presentations were the topic of this chapter. Covered were group presentation principles and group presentation formats.

CHAPTER 13

LEADERSHIP

Some Thoughts on Leadership

- Leadership is one of the most observed and least understood phenomena on earth. *James McGregor Burns*
- Of the good leaders the followers will say when the leaders have gone, "We could have done it ourselves." *Chinese proverb*
- Good followers make good leaders. *Anonymous*
- The good leader falls asleep at the beginning of the meeting and wakes up at the end and says "Yes." *Japanese aphorism*
- Unless you're the lead dog on the dogsled team, the view never changes. *Robert Crandell*

- Leadership is getting people to look beyond their own job descriptions for ways to improve and challenge the process. *Maureen Fries*
- Leadership is influence; nothing more, nothing less. *John Maxwell*
- Leadership is about change, not managing the status quo. It does not include doing that which you do today tomorrow. It means doing it differently or more or better, but not the way it was done today, and therein is the tension. *Stephen Wolf*
- Lead, follow, or get the hell out of the way. *Col. Oliver North*

As stated above, leadership is one of the most observed and least understood phenomena on earth. In this chapter we will look at a number of perspectives on leadership, acknowledging that we will not resolve the mysteries about leadership. Instead, the perspectives provided here will enable us to observe leadership behaviors more intelligently, and, in the process, help us improve our own leadership behaviors.

Definition

Leadership refers to the influential behaviors of one that bring about good followership, compliance, and superior performance in others. *Followership* does not mean a mindless, lock-step kind of following. Instead it suggests that the follower adopts the goals and visions of the leader and works toward achieving those goals and visions. To be a leader requires that followers *comply* with your directives at some level. The level may be basic and concrete (mow the lawn before noon) or abstract (suggest several philosophical approaches to elementary education in your next report). Leaders, if they are leaders, bring out *superior performances* in their followers. It should be apparent that the leadership role does not belong to any one person even if one person is designated the leader.

Leadership skills can be exhibited by any one at any time. Very dramatic examples of this have been reported in wartime where in a battle after the commissioned officers have been killed the "lowly" 19-year-old privates suddenly take over and exhibit leadership skills totally unexpected. The privates' leadership skills were there but lay latent. One of the fascinating people-watching pastimes is to look at people and assess their leadership capacities. How would they perform under stress, how would they manage people, can they quickly read a situation and come to a conclusion, and can they see the future in a way that no one else can, for example?

Are Good Leaders Born or Made?

At one time people believed that good leaders were born and not made or that leadership was a product of nature (genetic) and not nurture (experience and training). This approach to leadership was called the *traits approach* and evidence was gathered to support this approach. For example, if we can assume that intelligence, physical attractiveness, and certain personality characteristics are genetically determined to some extent, and we find that good leaders possess one or more of these traits, then we can make the argument that good leaders are born. The problem with this approach is that certain traits predicted leadership ability or at least were present in some good leaders but were not present in other good leaders. So the validity of the traits approach becomes questionable.

Leadership Styles

Another view on leadership is the *styles approach*. Here three leadership types have been postulated: the *authoritarian* leader, the *democratic* leader, and the *laissez-faire* leader.

Authoritarian Leadership

The Authoritarian Leadership Style

1. Sets goals individually.
2. Controls discussion with followers.
3. Sets policy and procedures unilaterally.
4. Dominates the interaction.
5. Personally directs the completion of tasks.
6. Provides infrequent positive feedback.
7. Exhibits poor listening skills.
8. Uses conflict for personal gain.

Consequences of Authoritarian Leadership

1. Increased productivity.
2. More accurate solutions when the leader is knowledgeable.
3. Enhanced performance on simple tasks and decreased performance on complex tasks.
4. Increased rebellion among the followers
5. Increased rate of quitting among followers.

Democratic Leadership

The Democratic Leadership Style

1. Involves followers in goal setting.
2. Facilitates discussion with followers.
3. Solicits input regarding the determination of policy and procedures.

4. Provides suggestions and alternatives for the completion of tasks.

5. Provides frequent positive feedback.

6. Exhibits good listening skills.

7. Mediates conflict for the good of the group.

Consequences Of Democratic Leadership

1. Fewer "dropouts."

2. Increased follower satisfaction

3. Increased follower participation.

4. Increased commitment to the group's goals.

5. Increased commitment to the group's decisions.

6. Increased innovative contributions from the members.

Laissez-Faire Leadership

The Laissez-Faire Leadership Style

1. Gives followers free rein to set their own goals.

2. Avoids discussion with followers.

3. Provides suggestions and opinions regarding tasks only when asked to do so.

4. Provides infrequent feedback of any kind.

5. Avoids conflict.

Consequences of Laissez-Faire Leadership

1. Decreased innovation.

2. Decreased motivation.

3. Decreased member satisfaction.

4. Decreased quality and quantity of output.

Discussion of the Leadership Styles

On a first reading of the characteristics of the three leadership styles, you might be motivated to discount the authoritarian and laissez-faire styles as too harsh or too anemic. The authoritarian style has been the style used in industrial economies where thousands of workers are working in large complexes. In such a mass operation there is a need for a top-down kind of leadership. The same leadership is the hallmark of the military where decisions must be made quickly, where someone must be in charge, and where there is no time for discussion. In other environments, of course, the authoritarian leader is an anachronism. Creative groups do not thrive with this kind of leadership. Creativity does not increase just because someone is shouting, "BE CREATIVE!"

For the most part the laissez-faire leader is an ineffective leader. Almost everyone has had the misfortune to be placed in a group with a laissez-faire leader at the helm. If members are not required to stay in the group as they might be at work, the group usually disintegrates. Readers of *Dilbert* can easily conjure up a laissez-faire leader. The only situation in which a group might thrive with a laissez-faire leader would be one where members were so motivated and dedicated to the goal that no active form of leadership was necessary. There are many anecdotal reports of computer specialists, for example, who are so driven by the challenge and fascination of the work that they require almost no supervision. They just need to be pointed in the right direction. In these cases one of the best things the leader can do is to stay out of the way.

Most of us prefer to be led by a democratic leader; we do not want to be just a cog in the machine but we want to contribute in all aspects of the group process. At the same time we do not want to be leaderless. The democratic leadership style provides a "happy medium" between the authoritarian and laissez-faire styles.

Leadership and Power

What are the types and sources of leaders' power?

- *Coercive Power* is based on the ability to administer punishment. This can be done by not approving pay raises, promotions, transfers, etc.
- *Reward Power* rests on the ability to give something of value to others. This can be perks, money, promotions, warmth, companionship, etc.
- *Legitimate Power* resides in the position rather than the person. Judges and police officers, for example, have legitimate power.
- *Expert Power* resides in the person and not the position. Physicians, lawyers, and systems analysts, for example, have expert power.
- *Referent Power* is role model power. Celebrities have referent power.

Of course many of us are put in leadership positions where we have virtually none of the above sources of power. This then creates the true test of leadership skill.

Theories Of Management

Related to the issue of leadership are theories of management. Since leaders, even leaders of small groups, are in a sense, managers, a discussion of these theories is appropriate here. Four theories will be discussed: McGregor's (1960) Theories X and Y, Ouchi's (1981) Theory Z, and Theory K, a theory being developed from an examination of today's organizational complexities.

The Theory X Manager

- Is responsible for organizing money, materials, equipment, and people in the interest of economic gain.
- Directs, motivates, and modifies the behaviors of employees.
- Perceives the average worker as non-motivated, irresponsible, and lacking ambition.
- Perceives the average worker as self-centered and indifferent to the group's goals and needs.
- Perceives the average worker as gullible, intellectually dull, and resistant to change.

The Theory Y Manager

- Is responsible for organizing money, materials, equipment, and people in the interest of economic gain.
- Directs, motivates, and modifies the behaviors of employees.
- Believes that employees are passive, non-motivated, irresponsible, lacking ambition, gullible, dull, and resistant to change because they have not been trained and because they lack experience in an organization.
- Believes that motivation and capacity for responsible and competent performances are present in people. Inside everyone is a good person trying to get out.
- Believes that the major task of a manager is to arrange the organization so people can become productive, self-motivated, and self-directed.

The Theory Z Manager

- Sees the organization as a family. All employees are family members.
- Assumes employment is for a lifetime just as a family relationship is for a lifetime.
- Assumes every employee has a responsibility to the family (organization) and the family members (other employees).
- Believes that in times of recession managers should sacrifice first.
- Spends an inordinate amount of time establishing and maintaining interpersonal relationships with the employees. Much of this time is used in consensus building.
- Believes in group promotions.
- Frowns on individual achievement and believes in the proverb, "The nail that sticks out must be hammered down."
- Believes that control should be informal, implicit, and employee internalized. Workers are controlled by allegiance to the group and they do not want to bring shame to the group by acting imprudently.

The Theory K Manager

- Works in an environment of uncertainty and chaos because of mergers, takeovers, reengineering, downsizing, globalization, and technological advances.
- Manages a workforce that has often been abruptly "gutted," early retired, dehired, or laid off, not necessarily because of poor job performance, but because of the chaos in the environment.
- Must manage workers who feel fear, guilt, pain, disorientation, exhilaration, empowerment, frustration, and confusion because on one day the workers are told they are the key component of the

organization and the next day they are told to clear their desks by four and leave. Moreover, when workers see their colleagues escorted into their offices by a security guard who watches them clean out their desks and then escorts them out of the building forever, the observing workers feel guilty for not having stopped this humiliating process.

- Managers are asked to cut costs but yet produce more, two goals that stand in seeming contradiction. This too contributes to the chaos.

Discussion Of The Theories of Management

The Theory X manager is much like the authoritarian leader, caring little about the followers or workers, and, in fact, taking a negative view of them. Getting the job done is primary and if you have to "bury the bodies" along the way, that's fine. Given this, it is sometimes perplexing to find that workers or followers of authoritarian leaders are satisfied with the leadership. The answer to why this happens is that many times authoritarian leaders are seen as fair: They hate everyone equally is one way to describe this fairness. Authoritarians can also create an *esprit de corps* among workers or followers. They are united against the "tyrant." Union members often bond together against management adversaries whom they see as authoritarian and Theory X-type in style.

The Theory Y manager and the democratic leader have some things in common. Both think that workers have potential and can contribute to the group or organizational effort. In organizational theory these two parties would be seen as human relations or human resources leaders, believing respectively that workers' feelings are important, and that workers are a key intellectual resource. Theory Y managers need to be somewhat like therapists, since part of their job is to bring out the good person that is assumed to be inside every worker. This can be a rewarding but frustrating effort, the frustration sometimes exceeding the reward level, and the Theory Y manager reverts to Theory X.

Theory Z has its roots in Japanese culture, a culture much more group oriented than western cultures. Efforts have been made to transfer the Theory Z approach into United States' companies with varying levels of success. As might be expected when these kinds of imports are attempted, usually some hybrid results, since you cannot import an entire cultural history. Most notable in the attempts to use the Theory Z approach in the United States is the benefit that results when managers begin to spend a great deal of time with the workers, getting their suggestions and hearing their problems. This has often been referred to as *management by walking around* (MBWA). The success of the MBWA style gives some support and credibility to Theory Y in that workers will respond if they are treated with respect and perceived as having the ability to contribute to the improvement of an operation.

Critics of Theory Z see this leadership style as paternalistic. The Theory Z leader is seen as the father and all the workers are children. Moreover, a dependency relationship is cultivated which results in workers becoming dependent upon the organization for a lifetime, similar to the child who never leaves home. Few workers in Type Z organizations strike out on their own. This might be perceived as a kind of betrayal by other group members and the departing member may indeed feel guilty for having "abandoned" the family. This is why there are few "lone rangers" in Theory Z cultures.

Counter-critics claim that this paternalistic view is too harsh and that to criticize another culture's practices is always hazardous. Quick judgment about a culture without knowing the history of that culture is shortsighted and may be somewhat ethnocentric. With the world shrinking because of rapid advances in technology we will probably see more and more hybrids, that is, management techniques that combine the best practices from many cultures.

To one degree or another all of us live in an environment of chaos and can sympathize with the Theory K manager. Even if we are not in a globally competitive business organization, individual lives have been thrown somewhat into chaos because of technology. Toffler (1971) identified the process three decades ago in the book, *Future Shock*, and things have only accelerated since then. A key defining characteristic of the Theory K work environment is that it is not so much manager against worker, or manager trying to bring out the good person that resides inside each worker, but instead, it is how can we all survive and be productive in the chaotic environment. Common examples of chaos are:

- When you finally learned everything you need to know about the current computer system and the system is reliable and dependable, the system is withdrawn, and another, unreliable but more advanced system is installed.

- A call to your local banker, once a person-to-person call, now involves an electronic menu of nine choices.

- Planning for a career once involved the consideration of a number of traditional jobs. But now it is difficult to say what the jobs will be even ten years from now because they do not exist at this time but they will come on stream.

- Manufacturers once had all the materials they needed stored in a warehouse adjacent to the fabricating facility. Now, however, there is no warehousing. Materials are delivered "on time" so they need to be handled only once. This complicates the whole manufacturing system and the system goes into chaos if there is some small glitch in the system, a bridge closure because of a vehicle accident, for example.

Of course counter-critics will say that technology has simplified life. You can order books, CDs, and other products on the web without facing the chaos of the shopping mall. But this type of activity seems to be the exception. For most people technology seems to have made life more chaotic. But here again there may be some positive value to chaos whether it is technology driven or from other sources related to corporate or organizational life. It builds character. People who learn to survive and thrive in chaos are probably better managers and group leaders. They know how to deal with stress, they learn to manage in stressful situations, and how to achieve goals in stressful and chaotic situations.

The Leader In Action

In this section we want to talk about more basic things. Specifically, we want to suggest things that you can do as a leader. There are three areas of emphasis. The first is the task area, the second is the interpersonal area, and the third is the administrative area. Good leaders should be able to perform well in each of these areas, or perform exceptionally well in one or two of the areas.

How Can A Leader Satisfy The Group's Task Needs?

- State the group's mission.
- Outline the steps that will lead the group to its goal.
- Predict problems that will arise.
- Diagnose problems when they do arise.
- Stimulate action.
- Create subgoals so the group can experience early and frequent successes.
- Provide clear directions.
- Provide positive feedback for goal-oriented behaviors.

How Can A Leader Satisfy The Group's Interpersonal Needs?

- Make sure each member has an opportunity to participate.
- Make sure members are aware of their obligation to participate.
- Resolve conflicts.
- Regulate discussions. Do not let anyone dominate.
- Be fair but at the same time know your members. There are differences among people. People are motivated in different ways.
- Provide positive feedback whenever it is appropriate

How Can A Leader Satisfy The Group's Administrative Needs?

- Prepare for every discussion.
- Plan an agenda.
- Begin every meeting by stating the purpose of the meeting.
- Periodically during a meeting, summarize the comments made and verbalize the consensual agreement among members.
- Know that the quicker the group moves through an agenda, the more the group experiences the feeling of success
- Start on time; end on time.

Characteristics of Admired Leaders

Kouzes and Posner (1997, p. 20) administered a questionnaire to over 20,000 people living on four continents: America, Asia, Europe, and Australia. The goal of their questionnaire research was to determine the characteristics of admired leaders. Twenty characteristics were presented to the questionnaire respondents for ranking. The following list shows the resultant rank order (from most admired to least admired of the characteristics):

- Honest
- Forward-looking
- Inspiring
- Competent,
- Fair-minded
- Supportive
- Broad-minded
- Intelligent
- Straightforward
- Dependable
- Courageous
- Cooperative
- Imaginative
- Caring
- Determined
- Mature
- Ambitious
- Loyal
- Self-Controlled
- Independent

The authors concluded that the majority of us admire and willingly follow leaders who are honest, forward-looking, inspiring and competent. This conclusion was based on the fact that these four characteristics were selected by the majority of respondents. The other 16 characteristics were selected less than 50% of the time.

Leaders on Leadership

Not all writing on leadership is produced by researchers. Leaders themselves contribute to the leadership literature. One such example is Maxwell (1998), a former minister who now owns a leadership and personal development consulting firm. Maxwell has presented what he calls the "irrefutable laws of leadership." In abbreviated form the "laws" are:

- Leadership ability determines a person's level of effectiveness.
- The true measure of leadership is influence, nothing more or less.
- Leadership develops daily, not in a day.
- Anyone can steer the ship, but it takes a leader to chart the course.
- When the real leader speaks, people listen.
- Trust is the foundation of leadership.
- People naturally follow leaders stronger than themselves.
- Leaders evaluate everything with a leadership bias.
- • Who you are is who you attract.
- Leaders touch a heart before they ask for a hand.
- A leader's potential is determined by those closest to him.
- Only secure leaders give power to others.
- It takes a leader to raise up a leader.
- People buy into the leader, *then* the vision.
- Leaders find a way for the team to win.
- Momentum is a leader's best friend.
- • Leaders understand that activity is not necessarily accomplishment.
- A leader must give up to go up.
- When to lead is as important as what to do and where to go.
- To add growth, lead followers; to multiply, lead leaders.
- A leader's lasting value is measured by succession.

For each of the laws Maxwell provides support usually in the form of anecdotes that involve well-known individuals.

Leadership and Goals

Perhaps the single best thing a leader can do is to have the group goal and the individual members' goals merge. The founder of Wal-Mart, the late Sam Walton, provides a good example for this assertion. Walton was famous for his pep talks to his associates. One such pep talk was described by Huey (1989). Sam begins his pep talk with a little rambling about his hunting, his new bird dog, and his new bird dog whistle which he demonstrates. He then gets down to business:

> I don't think any other retail company in the world could do what I'm going to propose to you. Its simple. It won't cost us anything. And I believe it would just work magic absolute magic on our customers, and our sales would escalate, and I think we'd just shoot past our Kmart friends in a year or two and probably Sears as well.

Sam proposes that whenever customers approach, the associates should look them in the eye, greet them, and ask to help. Sam says he understands that some associates are shy, but if you do what he suggests, "It would I'm sure, help you become a leader, it would help your personality develop, you would become more outgoing, and in time you might become manager of the store, you might become a department manager, you might become a district manager, or whatever you choose to be in the company. It will do wonders for you I guarantee it."

Then Sam asks the associates to raise their right hands and execute a pledge keeping in mind that "a promise we make is a promise we keep."

From this day forward, I solemnly promise and declare that every customer that comes within 10 feet of me I will smile, look them in the eye and greet them, so help me Sam.

Now let us examine Walton's speech. Is it just a little bit of "down home, corn pone, play it in the key of C, Mama"? Or is it a masterpiece? A case could be made for the latter. Walton skillfully merges group goals and individual goals. What are the goals of the associates?

Well, certainly their goals would include some if not all of the items on Sam's list: be less shy; become a leader; have a better personality; become more outgoing; and become a manager, department manager, or district manager. These goals associates can achieve if they simply smile, look customers in the eye, and greet them whenever the customers come within ten feet of them. Doing this will also help Wal-Mart reach its goal in that more sales and profits will be generated when customers are treated in a certain way.

In sum if you are ever placed in a leadership position, the first question you should ask yourself is, "How can I make the individual group members' goals and the group goals merge?"

Summary

We began this chapter by noting that leadership is one of the most observed and least understood phenomena on earth. And, the many facets of leadership discussed in the chapter lend support to the notation. Nonetheless, the complexity of a topic should not dampen our interest in the topic, particularly when that topic is so important.

Specifically addressed in this chapter were leadership styles, leadership and power, theories of management, leadership action, characteristics of admired leaders, leaders discussing leadership, and leadership and goals.

CHAPTER 14

COMPUTER-MEDIATED COM-
MUNICATION IN
GROUPS AND TEAMS

Because they are yoked to technology, computer-mediated communication (CMC) studies are recent, but their number has explosively increased, virtually paralleling the technology expansion. Early on, the concern was with media comparisons: Face-to-Face (FTF) communication compared with CMC. Because CMC is virtually stripped of nonverbal cues, cues important in the establishment and maintenance of interpersonal relationships, the computer medium was seen primarily as a task environment. And indeed this view has been supported by researchers (e.g., Hiltz, 1975; Hiltz, Johnson, & Agle, 1978; Hiltz, Johnson, &

Turoff, 1986; Rice & Love, 1987; Siegel, Dubrovsky, Kiesler, & Mcguire, 1986; and Sproull & Kiesler, 1986).

These supportive views were soon challenged by studies that produced contradictory findings, namely, that maintenance or interpersonally supportive utterances can emerge in CMC (e.g., Feldman, 1987; Ord, 1989; Weedman, 1991; Walther & Burgoon, 1992; Reid, 1993; Rheingold, 1993; and Walther, 1994). The contradictory findings suggest that the medium alone does not determine the nature of the interaction, that other variables are instrumental as well; for example, the task (Steinfield, 1986); the culture (Hiemstra, 1982); sustained vs one-shot interactions (Walther & Burgoon, 1992); anticipation of future interaction (Walther, 1994); and power and status (Saunders, Robey, & Vaverek, 1994).

Computer-Mediated Group Discussions

A number of investigators have examined computer-mediated group discussions (CMGDs). Yates (1996) and Werry (1996), for example, looked at the linguistic features of CMGDs, the former using a university computer conferencing group as a corpus and the latter an IRC (Internet Relay Chat) group. In general their findings were that CMGDs lie somewhere between spoken and written language. Attitudes toward CMGDs were analyzed by Korenman and Wyatt (1966) who found that users on LISTSERV's WMST-L forum felt like they were indeed interacting in a group.

Attitudes were also the concern of Ziv (1996) who did a case study on three workers' use of E-Mail. Ziv found that the workers were more comfortable with face-to-face group discussions (FTFGDs) than they were with E-Mail and that E-Mail did not flatten organizational hierarchies. Herring (1996) also was concerned about hierarchies, hypothesizing that CMGDs might allow those whose voices have been muted to be heard. Her results did not support her hypothesized ideal. Other researchers have investigated CMGD and FTFGDs with regard to productivity. Hollingshead, McGrath, & O'Conner (1993), for instance, found that

CMGDs lag FTFGDs on the productivity criterion, particularly when they are newly introduced or when there is high turnover in the groups. Straus and McGrath (1994), using three-person groups, found no difference in the quality of work in CMGDs and FTFGDs; however, FTFGDs were more productive. Finally, Olaniran, Savage, & Sorenson (1996) found that CMGDs were more productive than FTFGDs but that FTFGDs were found to be more satisfying.

Egolf et al. (1996a, 1996b) compared FTFGDs and CMGDs in a large Critical Incident study (details on the Critical Incident Technique are given in the next chapter). Eighteen, five-to-six member groups participated. Each group (comprised of undergraduates) engaged in two problem-solving discussions, one a FTFGD, the other a CMGD. The CMGDs were asynchronous meaning that messages were displayed on the participants' computer screens in the order in which they were receiver by the server (the central computer that received individual messages and distributed them to the group). Only one individual's message appeared at any one time. Therefore, when a group member was reading a message it may be that that message was composed and sent minutes before. The FTFGDs were synchronous in that members heard the message as it was being spoken.

In both discussions participants worked on consensus projects, one dealing with picking recipient candidates for two available donor hearts, and the other with selecting which of a series of life stressors should be used as a basis for awarding workers compensation. Subsequent to their participating in the two sessions, participants completed a survey based on the Critical Incident Technique

Six hundred fourteen critical incidents were extracted from the participants' completed surveys. The incidents were first divided into group maintenance and group task categories. Following Bales (1950), task incidents are those that relate to goal achievement and would include the giving or asking for opinions, orientations, suggestions, and so on. Maintenance incidents, on the other hand, are those that relate to the creation and maintenance of the emotional, interpersonal climate in the group. Included here would be those utterances that relate to agreement, disagreement, like and dislike, showing tension and tension release, and showing solidarity or antagonism. Next, the incidents were subdivided into the FTFGD and CMGD categories, and finally into incidents that tend to foster or not foster a good interpersonal climate in the group, and those that promoted or did not promote successful goal completion in the group.

Following are listings of the categories of incidents extracted from the participants' reports.

Category 1: Incidents In the FTFGDs That Fostered A Good Interpersonal Climate

- 73 incidents dealt with the presence of nonverbal messages in this mode.
- 19 incidents dealt with the greater level of participation in this mode.
- 12 incidents dealt with the greater ease of communication in this mode.

Category 2: Incidents in the FTFGDs That Did Not Foster A Good Interpersonal Climate

- 16 incidents dealt with the situation where one person can dominate in this mode.

Category 3: Incidents In The CMGDs That Fostered A Good Interpersonal Climate

- 63 incidents dealt with the fact that people can communicate anonymously in this mode. No one can make personal attacks.
- 59 incidents dealt with the fact that there is less pressure to conform in this mode.
- 26 incidents dealt with the fact that there is more honesty in this mode.
- 15 incidents found that there was less arguing in this mode and thus it was a more affable mode.
- 11 incidents revolved around the fact that there was no hierarchy in this mode.

Category 4: Incidents in the CMGDs That Did Not Foster A Good Interpersonal Climate

- None.

Category 5: Incidents In The FTFGDs That Promoted Successful Goal Achievement

- 23 incidents focused on this mode as being superior because it takes less time and thus it is an optimal mode.
- 16 incidents found the instant feedback to be a recommending feature of this mode.
- 13 incidents suggested that responsibilities of group members need not be as sustained in this mode and thus the mode is optimal because participants can relax.

Category 6: Incidents In The FTFGDs That Did Not Promote Successful Goal Achievement

- None.

Category 7: Incidents In The CMGDs That Promoted Successful Goal Achievement

- 33 incidents found this mode of discussion to be optimal simply because participants were in different places permitting them to concentrate more on the problem.
- 29 incidents suggested that this mode produced more thoughtful responses and thus a more optimal problem-solving group.
- 21 incidents assigned superiority to this mode because it produced a written record.
- 18 incidents suggested that this mode of discussion kept the group much more focused on the problem.
- 11 incidents found this mode to be the optimal approach because there were no interruptions.

Category 8: Incidents In The CMGDs That Did Not Promote Successful Goal Achievement

- 42 incidents suggested that this mode was inferior because it took inordinately more time.
- 40 incidents centered around the loss of effectiveness in this mode caused by delayed feedback.
- 37 incidents found that there was no real discussion of problems in this mode but just a barrage of suggestions.
- 20 incidents suggested that in this mode it is more difficult to settle on an organizational structure.
- 17 incidents found an inverse relationship between the effectiveness of this mode and problem or task difficulty.

The results of this study are both confirming and revealing. The results, for example, confirm both intuitive (e.g., Khoshafan & Buckiewicz, 1995) and empirical (e.g., Siegel et al. 1986; and Sproull & Kiesler, 1986) ideas about the absence of nonverbals in CMGDs.

Participants found the presence of nonverbal cues in the FTFGDs to foster a good interpersonal climate in the group, and by implication, their absence in the CMGDs to be a liability. The data also confirm the finding (e.g., Khoshafen & Buckiewicz, 1995) that in FTFGDs one person can dominate to the detriment of others.

The data reveal certain aspects of CMGDs. The researchers cited above, who claimed that CMGDs were stripped of nonverbal messages, believed that the group as a result became dedicated to the task by default because of the difficulty of sending socio-emotional-type messages. The data suggest that the CMGD mode allows or clears the way for the group to focus on the task. Participants reported incidents in high frequencies that demonstrated that this mode enabled them to be anonymous, that there was less pressure to conform, that there was more honesty, less arguing, and no evidence of hierarchy in this mode. Participants also thought that this mode produced more thoughtful responses and kept the group focused. Countering these incidents that recommended this mode as optimal were incidents that reported this mode as ineffective because it took more time, produced delayed feedback, and generated no real discussion.

At times there were contradictory findings. For example, 29 reported incidents suggested that CMGDs produced more thoughtful responses while 37 reported incidents suggested the opposite, that no real discussion took place.

Not unexpectedly the data suggest that neither mode is clearly the optimal mode for group discussion, and clearly that neither mode should be discarded. As a consequence, a time-sequenced blend of modes might be considered optimal. Perhaps problem-solving groups should begin with the CMGD mode. In this mode participants feel that they have the most freedom to report. All group members should experience this freedom.

At the same time members in problem-solving groups have socio-emotional or interpersonal needs. The focus cannot be exclusively on the task. A good recommendation, therefore, would be to do the CMGD sessions first and then conduct FTFGDs afterward. Doing this allows group members to meet one another face-to-face after they have interacted on the basis of their logic, their arguments, and their points of view; and before they have formed impressions based on physical appearance, gender, and status, for example

The above research project had participants interacting in the CMGD sessions in computer-equipped classrooms spread across a university campus. All participants were using the same transmission speeds. In doing CMGDs with students in an e-learning class where they participate from their homes, transmission speeds vary widely. Some students have rather slow modems while others have the much faster DSL and ISN lines. This makes even asynchronous communication somewhat choppy but aside from this choppiness the reports from the research project reported immediately above generally apply to the e-learning situation.

It is often suggested that if CMGD participants would equip their computers with web-cams (small inexpensive cameras attached to the computer), then important nonverbal messages could be transmitted as well. In addition to the words streaming on the screen, the faces of all the participants could be posted as well in a Hollywood Squares-type configuration. Most participants reject this idea. When they participate at home they want the freedom to be in any state of dress and appearance, to be eating, and so on.

There may be some remedy for not wanting to be seen as you are at home but still wanting to be seen nonetheless. Recently (Egolf, 2001) a new technology has emerged. A person is videotaped speaking a specially-prepared passage. This is called *enrollment*. Once enrolled the person's physical appearance (as it was on the day the person was enrolled), body movements, and speech can be synthesized by typing words on a computer. So it may be possible to be seen and heard "live," (elegantly dressed, with cheery expressions) in a CMGD while sitting at home in your PJs with a towel around your head typing on your computer.

Gender and CMGDs

The majority of studies on FTFGDs and gender have found that women are predominantly maintenance oriented (manifested in statements that create and maintain the social and emotional climate of the group) and men are predominantly task oriented (manifested in statements that lead to goal achievement). Whether these same results would be found in CMGDs has been a question that has interested a number of investigators.

Herring (1996), for example, compared participants' messages on two large Internet lists: LINGUIST and WMST (Women's Studies). The two lists differed in their gender make-up with WMST having an 88% female subscriber base and LINGUIST a 36% female base; women contributed approximately 88% of the messages to WMST but only 15% to LINGUIST. The list comparison permitted Herring to test for the effects of gender and lists and for the interaction between the two factors.

Herring found women and men interacting on both lists satisfied a need forsocial interaction, and that pure information exchange took second place to the social interaction. At the same time she found significant gender differences. Women's messages on both lists tended to be supportive in orientation while men's messages tended to oppose and criticize others. Finally, she found some evidence to support an interaction between the gender composition of the lists and interactional orientation; namely, participants tended to change their styles to resemble that of the dominant gender on the list.

Overall, then, Herring's research findings on CMGDs and gender essentially were the same as those found in studies on FTFGDs and gender. Herring reported that the participants in her CMGDs were not anonymous, and that there were hierarchical differences among her participants which too were public. Noting that Herring's participants were not anony-mous and that there were hierarchical differences among the participants, Egolf et al. (1996c) conducted two studies of CMGD and gender. In both studies all participants were anonymous.

In the first study, a Balesian analysis was performed on the utterances produced by two, mixed-sex, five-member, task groups. Results showed significant agreement in the rank-ordered frequencies with which the Balesian utterance types were used across group members, regardless of their gender, in both groups. This means that males did not make signifi-cantly more task utterances than females, and females did not make sig-nificantly more socio-emotional support utterances than males. In short, gender differences that were found in Herring's studies and in FTFGD studies were not found in the present study.

In the second study, 92 judges read transcripts of the CMGDs gener-ated in Study 1, in order to determine if the computer-mediated commu-nicators were female or male. One hundred thirty five conversational turns were judged. Judgment data showed that, overall, judges correctly identified the sex of the communicator only 51.66% of the time.

The two studies show that the conventional wisdom that women and men talk differently is not always correct. Given a problem to discuss and being able to discuss that problem anonymously in a CMGD seems to erase the expected gender differences.

Of interest in the CMGDs was the search for social information at the end of the discussions. When their tasks were completed and there was an imagined sigh of relief, participants began to type in messages such as, "Who is AMP19," "Who STR7," and so on. Once again the recommen-dation seems to be warranted that a good way to get good task perform-ance is to conduct a CMGD with the participants remaining anonymous and then follow this with an FTFGD or a social-chat-type CMGD. The latter can be a reward for the former.

Computer-Mediated Focus Groups

Egolf (1997a and 1997b) compared face-to-face-focus groups (FTFFGs) and computer-mediated focus groups (CMFGs). Eight groups of five or six members were randomly assigned to a FTFFG or a CMFG. All participants (upper-level undergraduates) were asked to prepare an individual statement on all of their educational experiences, from the time they entered school in first grade until the present. They were asked to think about the things that were instrumental in keeping them in school throughout the years. They were also asked to describe as many situations as possible where they became discouraged and wanted to quit school, and to tell who encouraged them to continue or what circumstances or situations helped them to continue.

The actual problem being investigated was, "How can a college or university retain students once they admit them?" The participants in the study were not informed of the problem being investigated until after all focus group discussions were completed. They were then debriefed.

Following the composition of the individual statements the focus group discussions began in both the FTFFGs and the CMFGs. The FTFFG discussions were transcribed and transcripts of the CMFGs were captured from the computer. These transcriptions were then analyzed and compared.

The results showed that both FTFFGs and CMFGs produced descriptive individual statements. The individual statements in the CMFGs were more disclosing than in the FTFFGs but in the focus group discussions the FTFFG participants seemed to disclose equally well. Both FTFFGs and CMFGs generated content in their discussions that was useful in solving the problem at hand. At times there were tears in the FTFFGs when, for example, participants talked about their parents getting divorced and how this affected their attitudes toward school. Similar observations could not be made of the CMFG participants, but the content of their transcripts suggested that there might have been tears on some keyboards.

Overall the study showed that productive and problem-solving CMFGs can be conducted.

Computer-Mediated Brainstorming

Connolly (1997) has provided a comprehensive evaluation of computer-mediated brainstorming (CMBS) and face-to-face brainstorming (FTFBS). Connolly concluded that FTFBS is ineffective for three reasons. First, participants are apprehensive; they are afraid of negative evaluations when they offer their ideas. Second, FTFBS permits social loafing; some participants do nothing for they know they will receive the same rewards as others. Third, there is the access problem; in FTFBS sessions only one person can speak at a time thus limiting the number of ideas generated in a given period of time.

On the other hand, Connolly found CMBS to be an effective generator of creative ideas. The reason for this seems to be that more people can generate ideas at the same time (supporting Osborne's notion reported in the problem-solving section that quantity produces quality) and thus more ideas can be produced in a given period of time than can be in FTFBS. The FTFBS limitation of only one person speaking at a time is avoided. Of great interest too was the fact that more ideas and more creative ideas were produced when the participants were anonymous. Once again the effect of anonymity was manifest.

Egolf (1998) reported on his studies with CMBS and found results in agreement with Connolly; specifically that CMBS can generate a large number of ideas in a given period of time, far in excess of that produced in FTFBS in the same time period. In Part II of the brainstorming technique (The Follow-Up Session) a computer-mediated analysis can be somewhat cumbersome in that only so many ideas can appear on the screen at the same time. However, it was found that this problem can be resolved if the list of ideas generated in Part I (the actual brainstorming session) is emailed to the idea evaluators who participate in Part II (the follow-up session) prior to the evaluation meeting.

Summary

CMGDs can be as efficacious as FTFGDs. This can include general problem-solving discussions, focus groups, and brainstorming. Brainstorming, in particular, seems to be amenable to computer mediation. In fact, CMBS seems to be superior to FTFBS in terms of the number of creative ideas produced. CMBS's superiority seems to be further elevated if the participants are anonymous. The anonymity factor surfaces also in, in general, CMGDs. Here, if participants remain anonymous, the reported linguistic differences between women and men participants seem to be erased and more productive work can be achieved as a result.

CHAPTER 15

EVALUATING GROUPS AND TEAMS

Often you want to evaluate the small group's or team's activities. You may want to do this for a number of reasons. It might be to better understand group and team dynamics, to identify group behaviors that lead to success or failure, to compare groups, or to assess individual contributions to the group effort. In this chapter we will look at a number of techniques that can be used to evaluate group and team performance. They are Bales' Interaction Process Analysis, Flanagan's Critical Incident Technique, Benne and Sheats' Role Analysis, the 360 technique, and rating scale techniques. The first three of the techniques are rather specific and the latter two are more general.

Bales' Interaction Process Analysis

When you use Bales' (1950) Interaction Process Analysis you transcribe the group interaction that you wish to analyze. You then mark this transcript in a specified way. The transcript provides the basic data for the analysis.

The marking of the transcript follows these steps. First, you mark the transcript with respect to turns. A *turn* consists of a group member's utterance from the time the member begins to speak until the time the member finishes the utterance. When one member finishes an utterance and another member begins to speak, then a second turn begins. Therefore, the first step is to segment the transcript into turns. Second, the turns are further segmented into acts. An *act* is a subsegment of a turn that can be viewed as a complete thought, is meaningful, and can stand by itself. A turn can have one or many acts. For example, if a group member says, "We should build a new school," this is a turn that contains only one act. If, on the other hand, the same group member says, "I think that we should build a new school and hire 40 more teachers," then you now have a turn with two acts: Act 1: build a new school; Act 2: hire 40 more teachers.

Once you have segmented the entire transcript down to the level of communication acts you are ready for the next step in the procedure.

After marking the transcript you categorize each communication act into one of twelve categories. The categories and their definitions follow.

Bales' Categories

1. *Seems Friendly*: Statements or acts that show solidarity, raise the self-esteem of others, raise the status of others, and show general affability.

2. *Dramatizes*: Statements or acts that show tension release, jokes, laughter, and general satisfaction.

3. *Agrees*: Statements or acts that show passive acceptance, understanding, concurrence, and compliance.

4. *Gives Suggestions*: Statements or acts that provide direction without depriving others of their authority.

5. *Gives Opinion*: Statements or acts that evaluate. These often begin with I think, I believe, In my opinion, It seems to me, etc.

6. *Gives Information*: Statements or acts that provide objective information, i.e., information that can be independently confirmed.

7. *Asks For Information*: Statements or acts that ask for confirmable information.

8. *Asks For Opinion*: Statements or acts that ask for evaluation and analysis.

9. *Asks For Suggestions*: Statements or acts that ask for direction and ways of acting.

10. *Disagrees:* Statements or acts that show passive rejection or lack of concurrence.

11. *Shows Tension*: Statements or acts that indicate a plea for help, a lack of comfort with the discussion, or an indication of impending withdrawal from the group.

12. *Seems Unfriendly*: Statements or acts that deflate the status and self-esteem of others and defend and assert one's own self.

When you have categorized each of the communication acts from the transcript into one of the twelve categories, you will have a profile of the group you are analyzing. By *profile* is meant that you will have the percentage (converted from the raw tallies) of the total number of acts that fall into each of Bales' 12 categories. Category 1, Category 2, Category 3, and so on through Category 12. You now can take this data and compare it to Bales' "Norms" (Littlejohn, 1978, p. 273). The norms are the general category percentages that functioning and successful task groups generate. Below are Bales' norms.

Bales' Norms

1. *Seems Friendly*: 3%
2. *Dramatizes*: 6%
3. *Agrees:* 11%
4. *Gives Suggestions*: 5%
5. *Gives Opinions*: 19%
6. *Gives Information*: 25%
7. *Asks For Information*: 5%
8. *Asks For Opinion*: 3%
9. *Asks For Suggestions*: 1%
10. *Disagrees:* 4%
11. *Shows Tension*: 5%
12. *Seems Unfriendly*: 3%

There are some things of note about Bales' norms. First, the majority of statements in a successful task group are task statements. Categories 4 through 9 are task categories having to do with giving and asking for information, opinions, and suggestions. Fifty-eight percent of the statements are in these categories while only thirty-two percent of the statements fall into Categories 1, 2, and 3; and 10, 11, 12, the socio-emotional or interpersonal categories. Thus, to be successful, a task group must concentrate on the task. Even an excess number of acts or statements in Categories 1, 2, and 3, the positive interpersonal categories, can be detrimental to the task group. The group, in short, would be focusing too much on social aspects.

Note too that the largest percentages are in categories 6 and 5, 25% and 19%, respectively. Therefore, just two categories account for 44% of the total statements in a successful task group.

Also to be noted is the fact that there are many more statements in the "giving" categories (Categories 4, 5, and 6) than in the "asking" categories

(Categories 7, 8, and 9). The total percentage for the former set is 49% and for the latter, 9%. There are two reasons for this: one is strategic and the other is psychological.

The *strategic* reason is that to solve problems you must have information, opinions, and suggestions. Therefore, task groups need to put a lot of information "on the table" prior to and during their deliberations if they are to be successful in solving the problem at hand. Given this, it is not surprising that the percentage loading on Categories 4, 5, and 6 is so high.

The *psychological* reason for the high loading in these two categories relates to personal power. Powerful people give information. Weak people ask for it. And, people do not want to be seen as weak so they tend to give information much more than they ask for it. People sometimes believe it when they are told, "We are here to help. If you have any questions, just ask." Why should you be skeptical if you hear this statement? Again, the questioner, particularly the persistent questioner, is seen as weak, not on top of things, a slow learner, and so on. One of my former students told me that when he started on his first job, a fellow employee pulled him aside and said, "You can ask questions around here, but never ask the same question twice and don't ask too many questions or you're history."

As you can probably surmise, doing a Bales analysis on a lengthy group session or on a series of sessions is a laborious process. You may want to perform an analysis to learn the system and get a better feel for it. But it is unreasonable to think that you would do the analysis routinely. Nonetheless, if you have a grasp of the technique, you can informally think about the group you are participating in or the group you are observing and say to yourself, "This group is within the norms" or "This group is not within the norms and, therefore, is ineffective and perhaps on the way to disintegration."

Flanagan's Critical Incident Technique

The *Critical Incident Technique* (Flanagan, 1974) is a procedure for identifying outstandingly effective and ineffective performances of an activity. If you can identify the behaviors that underlie outstandingly effective and ineffective performances, then you can *evaluate* people who perform certain activities, and you can improve your *training* procedures for people who will, in the future, perform the activities. It is important to note that the technique is not a specific tool for evaluating groups and teams; instead, it is a general technique that can be used to generate criteria for doing the evaluation. The technique has five major steps: Establishing The General Aim, Planning The Study, Collecting The Data, Analyzing The Data, and Using The Data.

Establishing The General Aim

If you are going to identify outstandingly effective performances of an activity you need to know the purpose or goal of the activity. Otherwise you have nothing to which you can anchor your observations. Flanagan noted that many people consider the purpose of an activity to be obvious, at least until you ask them. Consider leadership. What is the purpose or goal of a good leader? As suggested in the leadership chapter, there are many views of leadership and what a good leader should do. Therefore, if you are going to study an activity, you must know what the purpose of that activity is. Flanagan suggested that you might consult individually a few experts in the field and have each of them tell what the purpose of an activity is. From this survey a purpose or goal might be established.

Let us suppose you are going to do a Critical Incident Study on leadership for the purpose of establishing criteria for evaluating and training leaders. Let us assume that you concluded from a survey of experts that: **The purpose or goal of a small group or team leader is to guide the group to the successful completion of its goal.** This goal would not satisfy everyone, particularly those who believe leaders should elevate the self-concepts of the group members, for example. But suppose you adopt this goal. You are now ready for the next step in the Critical Incident Technique.

Planning The Study

In planning your Critical Incident Study you want to develop procedures that will provide you access to as many leadership behaviors as possible. Accordingly you develop a questionnaire that you can administer to people who have observed leaders. You will want to sample as many observers and leaders as possible. A typical Critical Incident questionnaire would cover the five points listed below.

1. *The purpose or goal of a small group or team leader is to guide the group to the successful completion of its goal.*
2. Now think of a time when you observed a small group or team leader who was *outstandingly effective* in achieving the above goal. Tell exactly what the leader *did* that indicated to you that the leader was *outstandingly effective.*
3. Describe the type of group in which this incident occurred.
4. Now think of a time when you observed a small group or team leader who was *outstandingly ineffective* in achieving the above goal. Tell exactly what the leader *did* that indicated to you that the leader was *outstandingly ineffective.*
5. Describe the type of group in which this incident occurred.

Note that the questionnaire uses the word "did." This is deliberate. You want the questionnaire to evoke behavioral descriptions of effective and ineffective leadership. You are less concerned with things like attitude or charisma. These attributes are more abstract and, therefore, difficult to use in any fair way to evaluate or to use in training. You are after the behaviors that can be observed.

Note, too, that the technique seeks outstandingly *effective* and *ineffective* examples. Flanagan believed that the best evaluative and training criteria are to be gleaned from the extremes of performance. Those extremes are the outstandingly effective and ineffective behaviors.

Having constructed your questionnaire, you are now ready to administer it to small group and team observers. The best observers would be those who have had experience in observing leaders; people who participate in groups and teams would be ideal as observers. You would recruit such observers and administer the questionnaire to them.

Collecting The Data

You could administer your questionnaire to groups using printed copies of the questionnaire or you could administer it face to face. Now, of course, the questionnaire could be administered over the web but here there is little control. A good compromise is to administer the questionnaire in groups using printed questionnaire booklets. You should administer the questionnaire and also be available to answer questions. When should you stop gathering data? Flanagan's answer was to stop when each 100 newly-completed questionnaires produce fewer than three new behavioral descriptions.

Analyzing The Data

Once the data has been collected it is analyzed by reading the questionnaire booklets and extracting *critical incidents*. A critical incident is a behavioral description that relates to the general aim or goal of an activity. In the tutorial example, a critical incident would be a description of a leader's behavior that was anchored to the goal of a good leader that we established for our study. For example, if an observer in your study said an outstandingly effective behavior observed was that the leader clearly outlined the steps we need to follow to reach our goal, then this observation would qualify as a critical incident. After all the critical incidents are extracted from the questionnaire booklets they are categorized. Usually the first order of categories is those incidents that fall into the effective category and those that fall into the ineffective category. Other category schemes can also be created. Once the categories are established you tally the frequency with which incidents fall in the respective categories.

Using The Data

After the critical incidents are extracted from the completed questionnaires and categorized you are ready to put the information to use. Let us assume, for example, that you want to evaluate leaders and, therefore, you need to construct a leadership evaluation tool. You can even give the tool a name. You can call it LEECH (The LEadership Evaluation CHecklist). LEECH could be a rather simple checklist made up of the critical incident categories that were discussed above. You would have effective and ineffective categories and you would tally how frequently the leader being evaluated exhibited behaviors falling into each of these two major categories and any subcategories you created. To use the incidents in training you would teach your prospective leaders to exhibit the effective behaviors and inhibit the ineffective ones.

These would be the most simple kinds of uses of the data but, at the same time, could be worthwhile in evaluation and training. There are, of course, other more sophisticated uses of the data: developing rating scales, screening examinations, proficiency examinations, performance evaluations, and diagnostic batteries, for example. Here you would still be using critical incidents in evaluating and training, but the development of the assessment tools would be much more sophisticated.

Hundreds of critical incident studies have been completed over the years. The studies have produced instruments used in evaluating and training airline and military pilots, air traffic controllers, bookkeepers, dentists, emergency room personnel, factory workers, teachers, police personnel, psychologists, research scientists, and supervisory personnel in a variety of organizations, for example. And if you have to undergo an annual review at work, it is quite possible that that interview was structured on the basis of the results of a number of critical incident studies.

Benne And Sheats' Role Analysis

After observing the roles people play in groups, Benne and Sheats (1958) factored the observed roles into three major categories, each major category having, in turn, a subset of categories. The Benne and Sheats role categories are as follows:

Roles People Play In Groups

Group Task Roles

1. *Initiator-Contributor:* The Initiator-Contributor offers new ideas to be considered by the group or states old ideas in a new way
2. *Information-Seeker:* The Information Seeker asks for clarification of ideas or requests evidence and facts.
3. *Opinion Seeker:* The Opinion Seeker asks for agreement or disagreement with ideas/proposals under consideration.
4. *Information Giver:* The Information Giver contributes relevant information.
5. *Opinion Giver:* The Opinion Giver offers opinions.
6. *Elaborator:* The Elaborator clarifies and further explains another member's ideas.
7. *Coordinator:* The Coordinator shows relationships among statements of fact or opinion from group members.
8. *Orienter:* The Orienter guides the discussion by keeping the group on track and moving the discussion along.

9. *Evaluator-Critic:* The Evaluator-Critic evaluates the adequacy of the group's information and accomplishments according to some set of standards.

10. *Energizer: The Energizer prods the members to action.*

11. *Procedural Technician:* The Procedural Technician handles routine tasks such as handouts, copies, room reservations, etc.

12. *Recorder:* The Recorder keeps track of the group's progress or takes minutes.

Group Maintenance Or Interpersonal Roles

1. *Encourager:* The Encourager provides support or shows acceptance of another member's idea or statement.

2. *Harmonizer:* The Harmonizer resolves conflict and reduces it, frequently with humor.

3. *Compromiser:* The Compromiser attempts to come up with an idea that will please everyone.

4. *Gatekeeper:* The Gatekeeper opens the channels of communication and promotes evenness of participation.

5. *Standard Setter:* The Standard Setter expresses standards for the group to achieve or applies standards in evaluating the group's progress.

6. *Group Observer:* The Group Observer evaluates the mood of the group.

7. *Follower:* The Follower accepts ideas of others and goes along with the group trends.

Self-Centered Roles

1. *Aggressor:* The Aggressor attacks other members in an effort to promote his or her own status.

2. *Blocker:* The Blocker opposes all ideas and refuses to cooperate.

3. *Recognition Seeker:* The Recognition Seeker boasts about past accomplishments, which are frequently irrelevant, usually in an attempt to gain sympathy.

4. *Self-Confessor:* The Self-Confessor engages in irrelevant discussion to work out personal feelings, mistakes, and problems.

5. *Party Person:* The Party Person displays a lack of involvement in the group through inappropriate humor or horseplay.

6. *Dominator:* The Dominator embarks on long monologues and tries to monopolize the group's time.

7. *Help Seeker:* The Help Seeker attempts to gain sympathy from other group members through expressions of insecurity or inadequacy.

8. *Special-Interest Pleader:* The Special-Interest Pleader brings in irrelevant information and argues increasingly from one point of view.

How can the role categories presented by Benne and Sheats be helpful in evaluating groups? Recall one of the themes that have run throughout this text. The theme is about task factors and maintenance or interpersonal factors. It was first mentioned in Chapter 1 when paradoxes were mentioned. The successful group must have the right mix of concern for the task and concern for the interpersonal climate of the group. Therefore, if you have a group that is not productive or is dysfunctional, there may be too many members who are task role players or too many who are maintenance or interpersonal role players. The functional and successful group needs role players from each area or people who can play both types of roles at different and appropriate times. Neither task role players nor interpersonal or maintenance role players are superior to one another. They are both necessary for the group to function well. They are complementary roles. It is the self-centered role players that the group can do without. Therefore, if a group is not succeeding or is dysfunctional, you should also look for the presence of self-centered role players.

Knowledge of Benne and Sheats' role analysis can also be helpful in selecting task group members whenever you are forming a group. In general, self-centered role players should be avoided. If you examine the self-centered roles listed above you will see that these people are indeed self-centered. They sap the energy from the group for selfish purposes; they should be avoided in forming task groups whenever possible. Otherwise, in forming task groups, you should try for the right mix of task role and maintenance role people with a slightly greater emphasis on task role individuals. The alternative is to select people who play both roles well. This should not be of the highest priority, however, since not all people play both roles well. A task role person who is extremely valuable at giving information, for example, may not provide good interpersonal support to the group. Another group member should be recruited to provide the interpersonal support.

The 360

The 360 evaluates a group by evaluating its individual members. 360 denotes full circle and this characterizes a technique that includes an evaluation of each group member by every other group member. Sometimes in organizations it also includes evaluations by all peers, superiors, and subordinates in the group member's environment. The evaluations can be quantitative (ranks or ratings) or in narrative form. In most cases the evaluations are delivered to group members with the specific evaluators remaining anonymous. This is particularly important if group members are to continue to work in harmony on future projects.

The 360 evaluation procedure assumes that a group effort and group success are very much dependent upon members doing their own jobs. Worry about your job first and do not worry about other members' contributions and everything will take care of itself. In the 360, members find out how well they have been doing their "group jobs."

The notion that teamwork consists of team members doing their own jobs and not worrying about others was reflected in a statement by Chuck Noll, former coach of the Pittsburgh Steelers, winner of four super bowls, and a member of the Pro Football Hall of Fame. When asked by an interviewer (Cheever, 1993), "You had a saying: whatever it takes. Is that your philosophy of life?" Noll replied:

> No. I think what it really did was describe teamwork. You do whatever you have to do to make the team function, and you don't worry about somebody else's contribution. It depends on whatever the challenge is because different people have different skills. So if you want to put it all together, you can't worry about measuring contribution, you can't worry about anybody else, you've got to get yourself focused and working. As a team, as a group, we can accomplish a heck of a lot more.

Rating Scales

A *rating scale* is an instrument wherein the rater indicates that an entity possesses more or less of something than that possessed by another or other similar entities. Rating scale procedures are probably the most pervasive quantitative evaluation techniques. They can be used to evaluate everything from sailing ships, to sealing wax, to groups. Although there are various types of rating scales, the most frequently used rating scale is called the *standard scale*. Suppose you were developing a rating scale for evaluating group leaders. The beginning part of the scale might look like this:

Instructions: use the following ratings for each of the items below.

1=Extremely Successful
2=Moderately Successful
3=Fairly Successful
4=Fairly Unsuccessful

5=Moderately Unsuccessful

6=Extremely Unsuccessful

In stating the group's mission the leader was: 1 2 3 4 5 6

In motivating group members the leader was: 1 2 3 4 5 6

In anticipating future problems the leader was: 1 2 3 4 5 6

Note that an even number of rating choices was used in the sample three-item rating scale. Does it make a difference if there is an odd number or even number? It does. An even number, forces raters to go to one side of the issue or the other. An odd number of choices gives them a "middle ground" or neutral rating which they can select.

How many choice points should you have? The answer to this is somewhat similar to how many people make up a small group. The number of choice points should be between five and nine. Fewer than five reveals little discrimination. If there are more than nine, people begin to *zone* the ratings, i.e., they "chunk" a 15-choice point scale into a five-point scale by chunking the 15 points into five sets of three each.

A very important consideration in constructing rating scales is the content of the items. This is a *validity* issue. Validity refers to whether or not a rating scale battery really measures what it is supposed to measure. If someone receives a very high rating on a leadership rating scale, for example, that person should indeed be a good leader if our rating scale is valid. This is a key question for you if you construct rating scales. In too many rating scales someone has literally just pulled things "out of the air." It is best if the content of the rating scale items comes from research. For example, many good rating scale items emerge from Critical Incident studies. And, if you look at the research of Bales, and of Benne and Sheats reported in abbreviated form above, you could probably generate some reasonably good rating scale items to evaluate aspects of small group communication. With the right content in the items, rating scales can be very helpful evaluative tools.

Technique Blends

Often evaluation techniques utilize a blend of methodologies. The 360, for example, can utilize rating scales, and the items for rating scales in turn are often derived from Critical Incident studies. Rating scale items could also be constructed from the information contained in Bales' and Benne and Sheats' categories as noted above.

Rating scales are very popular evaluation tools. They are understood by raters, they take little time to administer, and they produce quantitative data ready for statistical analysis by computer. Bales' and Flanagan's techniques are much more labor intensive since they produce qualitative linguistic data which first must be analyzed by humans. With both techniques humans must make judgments as they categorize either spoken or written reports.

Evaluations should be routine. They should be used not only when a group has failed but also when the group has succeeded. Moreover, evaluations should be conducted during the period of time the group is working on a task (these are sometimes called *formative evaluations*), and after the group has completed its task (these are sometimes called *summative evaluations*).

Summary

In this chapter we looked at a number of techniques for evaluating group performance. The techniques examined were Bales' Interaction Process Analysis, Flanagan's Critical Incident Technique, Benne and Sheats Role Analysis, The 360 technique, and rating scale techniques.

References

Asher, D. (2000). Discrimination: A weighty matter. *Psychology Today*, May/June, 14.

Bach, G.R. (1980). Marathon group therapy. In Herink, R. (Ed.), *The psychotherapy handbook*. NY: Meridian, 356-359.

Bales, R.F. (1950). *Interaction process analysis: A method for the study of small groups*. Chicago: The University of Chicago Press.

Bales, R.F. & Strodtbeck, F.L. (1951). Phases in group problem-solving. J. *Abnormal & Social Psychology*, 46, 485-495.

Barker, et al., (1980). An investigation of proportional time spent in various communication activities by college students. *J. of Applied Communication Research*. 8, 101-109.

Beebe, S.A. & Masterson, J.T. (2000). *Communicating in small groups: principles and practices* (6th ed.). NY: Addison Wesley Longman.

Benne, K. & Sheats, P. (1958). Functional roles of group members. *J. of Social Issues*, 4, 41-49.

Bennis, W.G. & Shepard, H.A. (1956). A theory of group development. *Human Relations*, 9, 415-437.

Berne, E. (1967). *Games People Play*. NY: Grove Press.

Bower, B. (1995a). Return of the group. *Science News*. 148, Nov. 18, 328-330.

Bower, B. (1995b). Ultrasocial Darwinism. *Science News*. 148, Nov. 25, 366-367.

Brady, D. (2000). An executive whose time has gone, *Business Week*. Aug. 28, 125.

Brilhart, J.K. (1978). *Effective Group Discussion* (3rd ed.). Dubuque, Iowa: Wm. C. Brown.

Buber, M. (1970). *Between Man and Man*. NY: Macmillan.

Carnegie, D. (1994) *How To Win Friends And Influence People*. NY: Pocket Books. This book was originally published in NY by Simon and Schuster in 1936.

Carroll, J.B. (Ed.) (1964). *Language Thought and Reality: Selected Writings of Benjamin Lee Whorf*. Cambridge, MA: The MIT Press.

Cheever, M. (1993). Whatever it takes. *Pittsburgh Magazine*. July.

Conlin, M. (2000). And, now the just-in-time employee. *Business Week*. Aug. 28, 169-170.

Deck, L.P. (1968). Buying brains by the inch. *The J. of College and University Personnel Association*, 19, 33-37.

Delbecq, A., Van de Ven, A., & Gustafson, D. (1975). *Group Techniques for Program Planning: A Guide to Nominal Group and Delphi Processes*. Glenview, IL: Scott, Foresman.

Durant, W. (1974). *The Story of Philosophy*. NY: Pocket Books.

Egolf, D. (2001). Augmenting communication with synthesized facial expressions: a controversial new technology. Proceedings of the 16th annual CSUN international conference on technology and disabilities. http://www.csun.edu/cod/conf2001/proceedings/0011egolf.html.

Egolf, D. (1998). Conducting the computer-mediated brainstorming session. Presentation at the annual Trenton computer conference, Edison, NJ.

Egolf, D. (1997a). Face-to-face and computer-mediated focus groups: comparisons and contrasts. Paper presented at the annual convention of the National Communication Association, Chicago, IL.

Egolf, D. (1997b). Analyzing the computer-mediated focus group. Paper presented at the annual convention of the National Communication Association, Chicago, IL.

Egolf, D., Gareis, J., Cohn, E., & Chester, S. (1996a). A comparison of two chronemic and proxemic permutations on their effectiveness in promoting optimal group discussion. Paper presented at the 87th annual convention of the Eastern Communication Association, NY, NY.

Egolf, D., Gareis, J., & Cohn, E. (1996b). Using technology to teach optimal group problem-solving skills. Paper presented at the 13th annual international conference on technology and education, New Orleans, LA.

Egolf, D., Gareis, J., Cohn, E., & Chester, S. (1996c). Computer-mediated group discussion and gender. Paper presented at the annual convention of the Speech Communication Association, San Diego, CA.

Egolf, D. & Corder, L. (1991). Height differences of low and high job status, female and male corporate employees. *Sex Roles.* 24, 5/6, 365-373.

Engleberg, I.N. & Wynn, D.R. (2000). *Working in Groups: Communication Principles and Strategies* (2nd Ed.). Boston: Houghton Mifflin.

Erikson, E. *Childhood and Society* (2nd Ed.). NY: Norton, 1963.

Feldman, M.S. (1987). Electronic mail and weak ties in organizations. *Office: Technology and People,* 3, 83-101.

Festinger, L. (1954). A theory of social comparison processes. *Human Relations.* 7, 117-140.

Festinger, L. (1950). Informing social communication. *Psychological Review.* 57, 271-282.

Fisher, A. (1970). Decision emergence phases in group decision-making. *Speech Monographs.* 37, 53-56.

Fisher, A. (1974). *Small Group Decision Making: Communication and the Group Process.* NY: McGraw-Hill.

Flanagan, J.C. (1974). *Measuring Human Performance.* Palo Alto, CA: The American Institutes for Research.

Frank, J. (1974). *Persuasion and Healing.* NY: Schocken Books.

Goffman, E. (1963). *Behavior in Public Places.* NY: Free Press.

Goffman, E. (1961). *Encounters*, NY: Bobbs-Merrill.

Goffman. E. (1959). *The Presentation of Self in Everyday Life*. Garden City, NY: Anchor Books.

Golembiewski, R. & Miller, G. (1980). T-groups. In Herink, R. (Ed.), *The Psychotherapy Handbook*. NY: Meridian, 652-655.

Gordon, T. (2000). *Parent Effectiveness Training*. NY: P.H. Wyden.

Gordon, T. (1986). *LET. Leader Effectiveness Training*. NY: Bantam Doubleday Dell.

Gordon, T. (1974). *TET. Teacher Effectiveness Training*. NY: P.H. Wyden.

Grigoriadis, V. (2001). The Me Generation. *New York Magazine*, July 9, 18-25.

Growth hormones given to normal kids. (1996). *Science News*. 150, Sept. 7, 154.

Herink, R. (1980). *The Psychotherapy Handbook*. NY: Meridian.

Herring, S. (1996). Two variants of an electronic message schema. In Herring, S. (Ed.), *Computer-Mediated Communication: Linguistic, Social, and Cross-Cultural Perspectives*, Philadelphia: John Benjamins, 1996, 81-108.

Hiemstra, G. (1982). Teleconferencing, concern for face and organizational culture. In M. Burgoon (Ed.), *Communication Yearbook* 6, 874-904. Beverly Hills, CA: Sage.

Hiltz, S.R. (1975). Communications and group decision making: Experimental evidence on the potential impact of computer conferencing (Research Rep. No. 2). Newark, NJ: New Jersey Institute of Technology, Computerized Conferencing and Communications Center.

Hiltz, S.R., Johnson, K., & Agle, G. (1978). Replicating Bales' problem solving experiments on a computerized conference: A pilot study (Research Rep. No. 8). Newark, NJ: New Jersey Institute of Technology, Computerized Conferencing and Communications Center.

Hiltz, S.R., Johnson, K., & Turoff, M. (1986). Experiment in group decision making: Communication process and outcome in face to face versus computerized conferences. *Human Communication Research*, 13, 225-252.

Hollingshead, A., McGrath, J., & O'Conner, K. (1993). Group task performance and communication technology: a longitudinal study of computer-mediated versus face-to-face work groups. *Small Group Research*, 24, 3, 307-333.

Huey, J. (1989). Wal-Mart: will it take over the world? *Fortune*, Jan. 30, 52-61.

Janis, I. (1982). *Groupthink* (2nd ed.). Boston: Houghton Mifflin Co.

Johnson, W. (1946). *People In Quandaries*. NY: Harper.

Keenan, F. (2001). Friendly spies on the net. *Business Week* e-biz. July 9, EB26-EB28.

Khoshafan, S. & Buckiewicz, M. (1995). *Introduction to Groupware, Workflow, and Workgroup Computing*. New York: John Wiley & Sons Inc.

Korenman, J. & Wyatt, N. (1996). Group dynamics in an e-mail forum. In Herring, S. (Ed.), *Computer-Mediated Communication: Linguistic, Social, and Cross-Cultural Perspectives,* *Philadelphia*: John Benjamins, 1996, 225-242.

Kouzes, J. & Posner, B. (1997). *The Leadership Challenge.* San Francisco: Jossey-Bass.

Kronholz, J. (1998). Chary schools tell teachers, "Don't touch, don't hug." *The Wall Street Journal.* May 28, B1.

Laing, R. et al. (1972). *Interpersonal perception: a theory and a method of research.* NY: Perennial Library.

Langlois, J. (1991). Facial diversity and infant preferences for attractive faces. *Developmental Psychology.* 27(1), 79-84.

Leary, T. (1953). The theory and measurement methodology of interpersonal communication. *Psychiatry,* 18.

Lee, L. (1995). Some employees just aren't suited for dressing down. *The Wall Street Journal,* 3, A3.

Lewin, K. (1948). *Resolving Social Conflicts: Selected Papers on Group Dynamics.* NY: Harper & Row.

Littlejohn, S. (1978). *Theories of Human Communication.* Columbus, OH: Charles E. Merrill.

Lumsden, G. & Lumsden, D. (2000). *Communicating In Groups and Teams: Sharing Leadership;.* Belmont, CA: Wadsworth/Thommson Learning.

Martin, J. (1998). How you speak shows where you rank (An interview with Sarah McGinty). *Fortune.* Feb. 2, 156.

Maslow, A. (1970). *Motivation and Personality* (2nd ed.). NY: Harper & Row.

McGinn, D. (2000). Mired in meetings. *Newsweek,* Oct. 16, 52-54.

McGregor, D. (1960). *The Human Side of the Enterprise.* NY: McGraw-Hill.

Maxwell, J. (1998). *The 21 Irrefutable Laws of Leadership.* Nashville: Thomas Nelson Publishers.

Miller, J. (1978). *The Body in Question.* NY: Random House.

Mintzberg, H. et al. (1976). The structure of unstructured decision processes.
Administrative Science Quarterly. 21, 246-275.

Newcomb, T. (1961). *The Acquaintance Process.* NY: Holt, Rinehart, & Winston.

Newcomb, T. (1953). An approach to the study of communication acts.
Psychological Review. 60, 393-404.

Olaniran, B., Savage, G., & Sorenson, R. (1996). Experimental and experiential approaches to teaching face-to-face and computer-mediated group discussion. *Communication Education*, 45 (3), 244(16).

Ord, J.G. (1989). Who's joking? The information system at play. *Interacting with Computers*, 1, 118-128.

Osborne, A. (1993). *Applied Imagination* (3rd Ed.). NY: Creative Education Foundation. This book was first published by Scribners (NY) in 1953.

Ouchi, W. (1981). *Theory Z.* NY: Avon Books.

Peters, T. (2000). The new wired world of work. *Business Week.* Aug. 28, 172-174.

Peters, T. (1993). Thriving in chaos. *Working Woman.* Sept., 102.

Popkin, R. & Stroll, A. (1956). *Philosophy Made Simple.* Garden City, NY: Doubleday & Co.

Reid, E. (1993). *Electronic chat: Social issues on Internet Relay Chat.* Media Information Australia, 62-70.

Rheingold, H. (1993). *The Virtual Community: Homesteading on the Electronic Frontier.* Reading, MA: Addison-Wesley.

Rice, R.E., & Love, G. (1987). Electronic emotion: Socio-emotional content in a computer-mediated network. *Communication Research*, 14, 85-108.

Robert, H. et al. (1990). *Robert's Rules of Order* (9th ed.). NY: Scott, Foresman.

Rogers, C. (1951). *Client Centered Therapy.* Boston: Houghton-Mifflin.

Saunders, C.S., Robey, D., & Vaverek, K. (1994). The persistence of status differentials in computer conferencing. *Human Communication Research*, 20, 443-472.

Schutz, W. (1966). *The Interpersonal Underground.* Palo Alto, CA: Science & Behavior.

Sherif, C. et al. (1965). *Attitude & Attitude Change: The Social Judgment-Involvement Approach.* Philadelphia: Saunders.

Siegel, J., Dubrovsky, V., Kiesler, S., & McGuire, T.W. (1986). Group processes in computer-mediated communication. *Organizational Behavior and Human Decision Processes*, 37, 157-187.

Smith, A. (1975). *Powers Of Mind.* NY: Random House, 269-284.

Sproull, L., & Kiesler, S. (1986). Reducing social context cues: Electronic mail in organizational communication. *Management Science*, 32, 1492-1512.

Steinfield, C.W. (1986). Computer-mediated communication in an organizational setting: Explaining task-related and socio-emotional uses. In M.L. McLaughlin (Ed.), *Communication Yearbook 9*, 777-804. Newbury Park, CA: Sage.

Straus, S & McGrath, J. (1994). Does the medium matter? The interaction of task type and technology on group performance and member reactions. *J. Applied Psychology*, 79, 1, 87(11).

Tauber, R. (1997). *Self-fulfilling Prophecy.* Westport, CT: Praeger Publishers.

Thibaut J. & Kelly, H. (1959). *The Social Psychology of Groups.* NY: Wiley.

Toffler, A. (1971). *Future Shock.* NY: Bantam Books.

Tuckman, B. (1965). Developmental sequences in small groups. *Psychological Bulletin.* 63, 384-399.

Walther, J.B. (1994). Anticipated ongoing interaction versus channel effects on relational communication in computer-mediated interaction. *Human Communication Research*, 20, 473-501.

Walther, J.B., & Burgoon, J.K. (1992). Relational communication in computer-mediated interaction. *Human Communication Research*, 19, 50-88.

Warner, W-J. (2000). Confessions of a control freak. *Fortune.* Sept. 4, 130-140.

Weedman, J. (1991). Task and non-task functions of a computer conference used in professional education: A measure of flexibility. *International Journal of Man-Machine Studies*, 34, 303-318.

Werry, C. (1996). Linguistic and interactional features of Internet Relay Chat. In Herring, S. (Ed.), *Computer-Mediated Communication: Linguistic, Social, and Cross-Cultural Perspectives*, Philadelphia: John Benjamins, 1996,
47-64.

Will, G. (1997). The last word. *Newsweek.* May 12, 92.

Yates, S. (1996). Oral and linguistic aspects of computer conferencing. In Herring, S. (Ed.), *Computer-Mediated Communication: Linguistic, Social, and Cross-Cultural Perspectives,* Philadelphia: John Benjamins, 1996, 29-46.

Ziv, O. (1996). Writing to work: How using e-mail can reflect technological and organizational change. In Herring, S. (Ed.), *Computer-Mediated Communication: Linguistic, Social, and Cross-Cultural Perspectives,* Philadelphia: John Benjamins, 1996, 243-264.

Printed in the United States
43625LVS00004B/271